I0843391

Time To Organize

Robert Mueller's Desperate and Phony Manafort-Cohen Blitz: Time To Organize

by Barbara Boyd

Aug. 22—For anyone thinking that the war against Robert Mueller is won and they can afford to not get out and organize their friends and neighbors to vote on Election Day, Tuesday, November 6th, the events of August 21, 2018, should have been a strong wakeup call, a hard kick in the rear end. Paul Manafort was convicted on eight counts of tax and bank fraud by a jury in Alexandria, Virginia. Donald Trump's longtime personal attorney, Michael Cohen, entered a guilty plea the same afternoon to a variety of tax and bank fraud counts as well as pleading to two Federal Election Campaign Act counts for payments he said he made at the direction of candidate Trump to silence two women claiming they had affairs with Donald Trump.

While the press goes wild in celebration and RESIST gloats, there is only one answer to this witch hunt: Get out, Get active, campaign on the LaRouche program to secure the future, mobilize a vote which will stun them all on November 6th. As we have said, again, and again, November 6th is a definitive day for the history of our country. With Donald Trump, great things are possible. If the insane Democrats triumph, the future gets very dark indeed. The various horrors of the Bush/Obama years and worse, will rise again, in full and awful bloom.

Paul Manafort: Low-Hanging Fruit

Paul Manafort committed a cardinal sin when he continued to support Victor Yanukovich in Ukraine against the 2014 British/American/neo-nazi coup which installed a corrupt puppet government in that country as part of a regime change operation aimed directly at Vladimir Putin and Russia. Ever since, he has been targeted in the way that people get targeted by

their weaknesses when they cross an arrogant, imperial power. As Lyndon LaRouche once said, there are really three ways—sex, family, money—by which people are corrupted, three major vehicles for compromising otherwise decent human beings.

The weaponizing of laws, the only way Robert Mueller has ever practiced, provides a fourth means—attack targets ruthlessly and selectively, let them stare at a sentence involving decades in prison. In typical Robert Mueller fashion, the Mueller indictment was overcharged; it exposed Manafort to 305 years in prison. Another indictment, involving the same conduct, but different crimes, is scheduled for trial in Washington, D.C. next month.

As Federal Judge T.S. Ellis commented, this prosecution has only one purpose: to terrorize Manafort into "singing" against Trump in order to save his own skin, to engage in the desperate acts by which witnesses "compose" rather than tell the truth. The pedestrian tax fraud and bank fraud charges implicate the types of things many in the D.C. lobbyist culture, with foreign clients in such locales as Israel, the Gulf States, and Saudi Arabia, engage in every day to minimize their taxes. It is the type of crime generally either settled with fines or with low jail sentences.

The difference is that Manafort had a target painted on his back from 2014 forward, and became an obsession for Mueller, who is establishing "credibility" by gathering easy scalps. The Manafort case had been under investigation and Justice Department lawyers were already active long before Robert Mueller ever became Special Counsel. Obama's Justice Department investigated Manafort's fairly notorious financial escapades and did nothing. The apparent balk was at the fact that numerous prominent Democratic Party lobbyists—

including Tony Podesta, the brother of John Podesta, Hillary Clinton's campaign chairman—were involved in the same Ukrainian lobbying activities and similar schemes.

With the effort to neutralize the results of the 2016 election, the case was revived, inclusive of information provided directly by Ukrainian intelligence agencies. Mueller picked up the already largely prepared case. It was the equivalent of "low hanging fruit." The Washington, D.C. indictment against Manafort involves a new and fairly unprecedented construction of the Foreign Agents Registration Act, violations of which are generally handled civilly. Mueller has referred the other lobbyists involved in Manafort's Ukraine activities, including Tony Podesta, to prosecutors in the Southern District of New York where many believe their transgressions will, again, be buried.

Michael Cohen: Not a Good Lawyer

Michael Cohen's law office files were rifled by FBI agents and prosecutors in the Southern District of New York in a stunning April raid which made national news and caused most sane individuals to ask whether it was safe now in the United States to ever tell a lawyer anything. Cohen apparently engaged in some very sketchy activities involving his taxi business and sought to exploit his former relation with the President after the campaign ended to make tons and tons of money in what appears to be a flaky influence peddling scheme. But, prosecutors really weren't all that interested in these transgressions. The headline here is that the lawyers in the Southern District of New York—many of whom are very bitter about Trump firing their former boss, U.S. Attorney and James Comey crony, Preet Bharara—want a role in framing the President.

If Cohen wanted out from under years in prison, he had to provide something against Trump. It turns out that Cohen had been taping his conversations with Trump, a violation of the most fundamental ethical obligations of a lawyer. Obviously terrified by his legal exposure, Cohen announced months ago that he was breaking with the President at the behest of his family and seeking a deal.

Cohen hired Clinton family lawyer Lanny Davis to orchestrate the deal. Davis' fawning loyalty to Hillary Clinton is legendary. His subservient and grandiose email correspondence with her, released in the various legal proceedings concerning her illegal email server, has been described, even in the liberal press, as "cringeworthy." Davis is also a completely devoted "third way" Democrat, beloved of the likes of Tony Blair and Joe Lieberman.

In his plea deal, Cohen backs the salacious and disgusting allegations of flat-out "porn star" and "exotic dancer," Stormy Daniels, and another woman, Karen McDougal, whose alleged sexual encounters with Donald Trump occurred years ago. These ladies, assisted by genuine scumbag lawyer and former Rahm Emanuel underling, Michael Avenatti, and the national news media, have been running a campaign for months, insisting that "hush money" paid to the two women by Cohen violated the Federal Election Campaign Act (FECA), and was a crime directed by Donald Trump.

Pursuit of these charges by the out-of-control Justice Department follows the complete failure of a similar case conducted by the DOJ against former Democratic presidential candidate John Edwards. Edwards was charged with FECA violations for arranging for hush money to be paid to hide an affair. A North Carolina jury acquitted him or otherwise hung on the counts in his indictment, which was almost universally seen, at the time, as a major abuse of prosecutorial power by Barack Obama's Justice Department. Most experienced legal observers do not believe that what Trump is alleged to have done is even a crime under the FECA.

So, are you really prepared to stand by and see a President taken down on the word of a porn star? Is that where we are? It should be obvious that the witch hunt can be ended, but only if we organize to determine that result. Make the next days our best days. Join our Campaign to Secure the Future!

Mid-Term Elections: Battle Between Paradigms, Not Parties

by Susan Kokinda

Aug. 26—In the countdown to November 6, 2018, one thing is clear: This will be a mid-term election unlike anything seen in the post-war period. Far from being a battle between the Democratic and Republican parties, what is playing out is a battle between the old imperial policies of war, globalization, and economic destruction, versus the emerging new policies of peaceful cooperation among sovereign nations, for the betterment of mankind.

Would that the November ballots gave voters a column for the old paradigm and a column for the new paradigm. They will not. Except in Texas and South Dakota, where LaRouche PAC-endorsed independent candidates are on the ballot, the columns will largely be defined in party terms. The LaRouche Political Action Committee has announced a national campaign to bring the real battle into focus and to challenge citizens to cast their votes from the strategic high ground.

On August 16, LaRouche PAC issued a national leaflet, entitled "Countdown to the Most Consequential 2018 Mid-Term Elections. We Must Take Charge Now!" The leaflet states, "This will be the most consequential election of our lifetimes. If the current crop of crazy-'Resist' Democrats takes the House, and the present, equally crazy free-trade, new Cold War loving faction of the Republicans joins them, President Trump will be impeached and the policies of George W. Bush,

Barack Obama, and Hillary Clinton, and worse, will re-emerge, triumphant. The world will be back on a course for war with Russia and China—a war which the human race will not survive."

The crazy-"Resist" Democrats and the equally crazy Cold War Republicans are both the political playthings of the modern day British imperial system, which is hoping to bring the United States back into its fold and save its dying system, by removing or crippling President Donald Trump. Most of the ground level anti-Trump politicos are as hysterical as they are clueless about what is bringing their world down. One of the most effective tools that a citizen has in dealing with the anti-Trump frenzy and defeating it is to understand what is driving it.

EIR Founder Lyndon LaRouche has put forward the proposition that an alliance of the four most powerful nations on the planet—the United States, Russia, China, India—would be sufficient to challenge and shut down the supranational British imperial system and replace it with a revived Bretton Woods credit system. Go back to the turn of the century, the chances were remote. Russia was being looted by the western bankers under the Yeltsin regime. China was recovering from the Cultural Revolution. India had suffered the loss, through assassination, of two Prime ministers, Indira Gandhi and, then, her son, Rajiv Gandhi. The United States was under a Clinton presidency besieged by Wall Street.

But Lyndon LaRouche has lived his life, knowing the power of putting the right ideas out into the universe, if not for the present, for the future.

Today, in 2018, the Four Power Alliance which he proposed then, could now become the dominant planetary reality. Russia, China, and India are increasingly in sync, through the spirit of the New Silk Road. President Trump has forged a relationship with China's President Xi Jinping. And when Trump finally met with Russia's Vladimir Putin—well, let's just say, the Empire struck back. The fury of the assault on the President, following the Helsinki Summit, is the real marker for what is at stake in 2018.

Those trying to prevent the election of an "impeachment Congress" will make a fatal mistake if they think the battle lines have anything to do with party. The unprecedented nature of the attacks on Donald Trump and the drive to unseat him are being driven by a desperate British imperial system, which knows how close it is to being overpowered—for the first time in history.

Going Door-to-Door with This Message

LaRouche PAC organizers on the ground in key Midwest industrial states, such as Michigan and Ohio, report that it is not party fault lines which reverberate among the Trump base. For one, they already know they can't trust the Republican Party. In fact, at the August 25 Michigan State Republican convention, Republican delegates were openly saying they didn't trust the Republican Party! And, at the huge Columbus, Ohio rally, addressed by President Trump on August 4, LPAC organizers found tremendous openness on the substantive questions of dealing with Wall Street's about-to-burst financial bubble and relations with Russia.

Two "good old boys" at the rally found themselves in the middle of a political firestorm because they designed and wore t-shirts that said, "I'd rather be Russian than Democrat." Neither one of them is on the Internet, so they were a little stunned to experience the ensuing reaction. Photos of them went viral, and one of them found a reporter camped on his front lawn. The other said, "I've been accused of treason, called a traitor and a Russian bot … well, maybe I'm just a Russian hillbilly." Not exactly your father's RNC Republican.

It is within these shifting political sands, that LaRouche PAC's *2018 Campaign to Win the Future* challenges citizens to "take charge now" and to fight from the high ground of a new paradigm replacing the old.

That was already implicit in the 2016 Trump victory. The two big game-changing policies upon which Donald Trump won the 2016 election were: first, his commitment to work with Russia, China, and other nations to end decades of perpetual warfare; and second, his commitment to end globalization and rebuild the U.S. economy and labor force. That is what brought blue-collar Democrats and independents over to the Trump side, and delivered the election.

But a mere rerun of 2016 will not be sufficient, not with an enemy pushing the extremes of hate-filled vitriol and demonization. What was implicit in 2016 must become explicit in 2018. The LaRouche PAC statement spells out the pledges to which voters must hold their candidates and themselves:

> First, stop the impeachment drive.
> Second, understand and fight for Lyndon LaRouche's full program for economic recovery.
> And, third, "work with Russia and China and other nations on areas of mutual interest, particularly conquering terrorism, joint ventures to develop infrastructure for the world's developing economies, and exploring space. President Trump has attempted this program for peace. He has been blocked at every turn by the City of London and Wall Street and politicians who profit from perpetual war and the cheap labor regimes of globalization and free trade."

LaRouche PAC organizers have begun distributing the leaflet at political gatherings. Local political officials and citizens are sharing it on social media, discussing it with their networks and committing to go door-to-door in their neighborhoods.

Case Study: Michigan's 11th CD

Michigan was one of the key, swing states in the Midwest which delivered the Presidency to Donald Trump. As one Trump supporter said to me recently, "the minute I saw Trump had won Michigan, I went to bed. I knew we had it." Voters in traditional blue collar districts continued to support their incumbent Democratic Congressmen, but cast their votes for Donald Trump in the Presidential election. Translating that national political shift into local Congressional races is not a given.

Michigan's 11th Congressional District (made up of the western suburbs of the Detroit metropolitan area) features a race for an open seat in Congress, a race which is already drawing national focus. Lena Epstein, a Trump Republican, is running against Haley Stevens, who chaired Barack Obama's auto task force. Besides being two women running against each other, in this "the year of the woman," the contrast between the new Trump insurgency and the old paradigm politics of the Obama/Clinton Democratic Party couldn't be clearer. But, look at the numbers: The turnout in the Democratic primary in the district was 4,000 votes more than the Republican turnout (both primaries were hotly contested). And, state-wide, 140,000 more Democrats than Republicans voted in the August primary.

The mission that LaRouche PAC has taken on, especially in key districts such as this one, is to ensure that voters understand the historic importance of this election, and do not go on a partisan-auto-pilot and end up with an impeachment Congress committed to war and Wall Street.

LaRouche PAC has a unique advantage in the 11th. In 2012, LaRouche PAC-endorsed candidate Bill Roberts ran in the Democratic Congressional primary, calling for Barack Obama's impeachment. He won 40 percent of the Democratic vote. Besides his signature "calling-card" posters of Obama with a Hitler mustache, Roberts prominently featured a return to the economic development policies of Franklin Roosevelt and John Kennedy. Roberts recalled getting petition signatures in one area: "All I had to say to people is that I'm a Democrat who wants to impeach Obama and rebuild the country and people would sign up." Those Democrats who voted for him are the swing base which must be activated and mobilized around the pledges spelled out in the LaRouche PAC statement.

And so it must be around the country. As the statement says, "What if the citizens of our country actually take charge—assuming the role that our Constitution envisions for them? What if we educate ourselves and tie our vote to a program which can actually restore this nation's greatness and ensure that an ever better and happier life is lived by our children? What if we tell any politician that our vote is based on their running on and implementing this program and nothing else? What if we, together, build a movement based on this pledge? Only such a movement can actually achieve the dramatic change for which citizens voted in the 2016 elections. If you think President Trump, backed by a 'silent majority' and forced to compromise for pure political survival, can do this, you have not grasped the actual situation."

Unite the World to Stop the British False Flag Chemical Attack in Syria

Aug. 28—Over the past three days, the Russian and the Syrian governments have exposed the intention of the British-backed terrorists in Syria, together with their "White Helmet" terrorist support apparatus, to stage a fake chemical weapon attack, film the White Helmets "saving" the victims, blast the videos around the world on fake news outlets, and induce President Trump to allow the war party to unleash a missile and air assault on Syria. It worked twice before, although Trump restricted the attacks to minor, limited strikes, with few casualties. However, now that ISIS has largely been defeated by the Syrian army, the British would like to provoke a wider war, both to prevent President Trump from carrying out his intention to withdraw U.S. forces from Syria, and to destroy the effort by both Presidents Trump and Putin to bring the U.S. and Russia into a friendly and cooperative relationship. In the eyes of the British Empire, the Helsinki Summit between Trump and Putin marked a deadly threat to that Empire.

Let there be no doubt: The British would vastly prefer a thermonuclear showdown, or even a thermonuclear war, between the United States and Russia, rather than see the imperial division of the world between East and West torn down. The power of the City of London and its Wall Street subsidiary depends absolutely on that division.

The first fake chemical attack in Syria took place in April 2017, while Trump was meeting with Xi Jinping in Florida, and was aimed at undermining Trump's personal cooperation with China's leader. The second attack came in April of this year, based on a White Helmet video which was proven by multiple witnesses, and even the testimony of the supposed "victims" themselves, to have been completely staged by the White Helmets.

The difference now is that the Russians and the Syrians have the evidence ahead of the fake chemical weapons attack, and have made it public, calling on the world to stop it. Russian Defense Ministry spokesman Gen. Igor Konashenkov told the press on Aug. 25: "To carry out the alleged 'chemical attack' in the city of Jisr al-Shugur in the province of Idlib, militants from the Tahrir al-Sham organization [Jabhat al Nusra in Syria, which is Al-Qaeda]…, had delivered eight tankers with chlorine to a village a few kilometers from Jisr al-Shugur. This provocation, with the active participation of the British special services, will serve as another pretext for the U.S., U.K., and France to conduct a missile strike on the Syrian government and economic facilities." He identified both the White Helmets and the Olive Group, a 5,000-strong British mercenary organization based in Abu Dhabi, as active participants in preparing the provocation.

In 2013, when the British claimed, without evidence, that Assad was using chemical weapons, President Obama ordered preparation for a full-scale military assault on Syria. Only the mass mobilization of the citizenry forced Obama to back down, after an outcry in opposition to yet another illegal and genocidal war against a Southwest Asian country which was no threat to us, and which in fact was staunchly anti-terrorist.

A similar mobilization today can and must prevent the current British plan for war. The fact that President Trump, unlike Obama, is opposed to regime change, wants to pull out of Syria as soon as ISIS is fully eliminated, and wants the U.S. and Russia to collaborate in this and other tasks, means that exposing this British provocation will also greatly contribute to stopping the British coup attempt against Trump through the Mueller "Russiagate" witch hunt.

In fact, President Trump was elected precisely because he is intent on breaking the "Special Relationship" with the British, a relationship which has turned the U.S. into a post-industrial junk heap, with a drugged up and demoralized population and a policy of permanent warfare. The LaRouche movement knows what is needed to make Trump a great President and to truly make America great again: He must be liberated from the coup attempt, freeing him to join with Russia, China and India in a New Bretton Woods agreement, to put the Western financial system through bankruptcy proceedings and restore the industrial economies of the West, in league with the New Silk Road development of the entire world. Unless the United States takes that dramatic step, there is no possibility for the world to avoid disaster—but the United States cannot take that step if Trump is brought down by the war party.

The New Paradigm is within our grasp—if we rise to the moment as a human race, to wipe geopolitics and Empire from the face of the Earth.

EIR Contents

www.larouchepub.com   Volume 45, Number 35, August 31, 2018

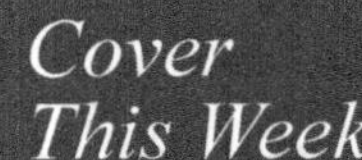

Cover This Week

The Midnight Ride of Paul Revere

BOOK REVIEW

What Is True Strategic Intelligence? The Case of the American Revolution

by Dean Andromidas

Spies, Patriots, and Traitors: American Intelligence in the Revolutionary War
Kenneth A. Daigler
Washington: Georgetown University Press, 2014
Paperback, 336 pages, $23.50

Aug. 25—Although on the bookshelves for nearly four years, the book under review comes at a very timely point in our history. The unprecedented political compromising of U.S. intelligence institutions over recent years has reached the point that the leadership of those institutions now stands accused of running nothing less than a coup against the sitting president, going beyond even the "military industrial complex" about which President Dwight Eisenhower so earnestly warned the citizens of this country. The rubber-stamp approval, by this same leadership, of the claim that Russia influenced the outcome of an American presidential election would make even warmonger Paul Nitze cringe with embarrassment.

Therefore, for the sake of the country, and especially for the thousands of professional intelligence and security officers who have dedicated their lives, often at great personal risk to their very lives, a reform is needed that looks towards redefining—or perhaps better said, reasserting—the mission of the intelligence community for the future security of this nation. When one speaks of "security," it is rightly not only about the danger of terrorism and aggression, but also about the opportunities that could benefit the nation. Indeed, while the mission of the intelligence community is to provide timely intelligence and analysis to the Presidential institutions to safeguard the nation, it also needs—and perhaps even

more importantly—to provide competent intelligence and analysis in the tradition of Sherman Kent's 1949 book, *Strategic Intelligence for American World Policy*. In the latter case, such an important development as the Belt and Road Initiative of China demands competent analysis, to present its great potential for the United States— rather than the inept presentation of it as a geopolitical threat.

A Needed Forward Looking Reform

The formulation of a forward-looking reform always requires reexamination and an assessment of the past, to discover the strengths and weaknesses, as well as the principles, of past performance. The examination of the intelligence activities of the American Revolution is the obvious beginning. Therefore, *Spies, Patriots, and Traitors* serves as a very good beginning for this task. Moreover its author, Kenneth Daigler, brings to the task more than three decades of experience as a retired officer of the Central Intelligence Agency. He examines the topic, not only as an historian, but as a professionally trained intelligence officer who can identify and assess American capabilities and the competence of American tradecraft.

Indeed, Daigler draws a parallel between the Sons of Liberty and the leaders of the fight for American independence, and the United Front of the Bolsheviks:

A united front organization is a principal tool for political and social organization. The term first came into use after the Bolshevik Revolution, but the general principles behind it are much older. It espouses a broad and somewhat general objective to a large number of groups and individuals willing to claim some connection to it. But its leadership usually has a more specific set of objectives … often more radical than the general membership realizes. Within this context, it can also be an effective operational tool for political action, one of the intelligence disciplines of covert action in the intelligence discipline. The Sons of Liberty's objective was to create a mass movement that first opposed specific British policies and then promoted political independence. While current national security emphasis on counter terrorism focuses on the paramilitary aspect of covert action, the other two basic elements—propaganda and political action—have a long tradition of use within the American intelligence community.

Daigler shows that American revolutionary "covert action" could at time be as ruthless as that of the Bolsheviks.

Daigler identifies the founders of American intelligence as George Washington, John Jay, and Benjamin Franklin, who are also three of the principal founders of our republic and framers of our constitution. Washington is identified as the founder of foreign intelligence, John Jay, counterintelligence and Benjamin Franklin, covert action.

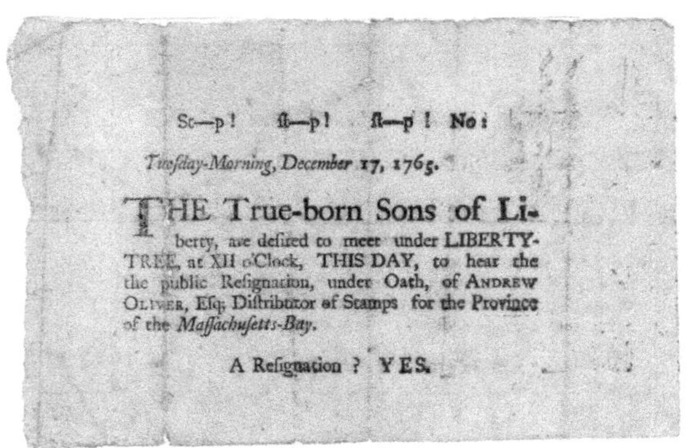

Massachusetts Historical Society

Broadside, calling for "Sons of Liberty" members to gather, Dec. 17, 1765.

George Washington

The most effective handling of the subject is his discussion of Washington as a practitioner and consumer of intelligence. Indeed Washington demonstrated a genius without which the United States might never have come into being.

Daigler ably documents Washington's ability to organize intelligence gathering networks, at both the tactical and strategic levels, even penetrating the British high command in New York to a degree that should amaze the reader, given his other responsibilities for organizing, directing, and supplying the continental army under extraordinarily challenging conditions, to the say the least.

More important, the author details how Washington was able to use that intelligence. Two operations stand out. First, Washington's famous Christmas Eve crossing of the Delaware to steal a victory over the Hessian mercenary forces, which not only gave a much needed boost to American morale, but was also a serious defeat of the British forces, which electrified public opinion on the other battlefield, Europe, especially in France, Germany, Russia, and of course in Britain itself.

The second demonstration of Washington's genius that is well documented in the book before us, is the grand deception operation leading to the defeat of Cornwallis at Yorktown. Many revolutionary war histories give a cursory ac-

Engraving by the Illman Brothers

Commander-in-Chief George Washington leads the Continentals to victory against Hessian mercenaries at Trenton, Dec. 26, 1776.

Detail from painting by Gilbert Stuart

President George Washington, March 20, 1797, 16 days after the end of his second term.

Painting by John Trumbull

British lord, Lt.-Gen. Cornwallis surrenders to the Continental Army led by General Washington and French troops led by Rochambeau, after the Battle of Yorktown, Oct. 19, 1781.

orchestrated conspiracies using colonists loyal to the British Crown is very timely. He relates how Jay, through his chairmanship of the Committee and the "First Commission for detecting conspiracies" was able to penetrate loyalist bands, particularly in the Hudson River Valley, with his agents.

As Daigler correctly points out, in a revolution, especially where principle is at issue, the line between friend and foe often falls across personal friendship. Such a case is that of Jay and his personal friend who, when he refused to take an oath of allegiance, was forced to withdraw behind British lines. Jay wrote to him, "Your judgment, and consequently, your Conscience, differed from mine on a very important Question. But though as an independent American, I consider all who were not for us, and You among the Rest, as against us, yet be assured that John Jay did not cease to be a friend to Peter Van Schaack."

It is a chapter one wishes were longer.

count of how Washington deceived General Clinton, Britain's commander-in-chief of its forces in America, into believing he was preparing against a combined American and French attack on New York. The deception was so complete that the British commander refused to send reinforcements to Cornwallis in Yorktown. Daigler has carefully and thoroughly detailed how Washington orchestrated this multi-leveled deception including setting up dummy supply depots and troop movements, and planting disinformation directly with Clinton himself through American penetration of his headquarters with double agents. It is a story well worth reading.

John Jay as Counterintelligence Officer

Not so well known is the role of John Jay as the revolution's counterintelligence officer. In today's world, in which counterintelligence—in the name of fighting terrorism—is seen as crossing the line of individuals' constitutionally guaranteed civil rights, Daigler's review of the way John Jay handled British-

Franklin and True Strategic Intelligence

The weakest section of the book is on Benjamin Franklin, whom Daigler identifies as the progenitor of covert action. This included organizing the purchase of weapons and ammunition, and the recruitment of European professional military officers. It also included the naval operations of John Paul Jones. Jones deployed privateers to seize British merchant ships and sold the prize ships to pay for military equipment. Covert naval operations included a plan for the invasion of England by joint action of John Paul Jones and the Marquis de Lafayette. Although the invasion was never carried out, a bold raid on the small English port of White-

Painting by John Trumbull

John Jay, around 1793.

haven by John Paul Jones, while of little material effect, was nonetheless a masterpiece of psychological warfare.

The author faults Franklin for counterintelligence and security failures, pointing to the fact that one of his own commissioners in Paris was in the pay of the British. He quotes Franklin himself saying he saw no point to hunting spies within his circle as he had nothing to hide. Daigler dismisses Franklin's attitude as "ingenuous."

Here it is not Franklin who is "ingenuous" but the author, because he fails to see that Franklin is operating on an entirely higher plane then the author appears to understand. While the choice of Arthur Lee, a paid British agent, and Silas Deane, a man who had a hard time separating duty from business, were poor choices, Franklin clearly understood the hopelessness of keeping secrets in countries and societies like France, Britain, and other European monarchies. He, without doubt, could easily imagine that anything he told his French allies would be reported to the British ambassador in Paris within hours.

Benjamin Franklin's Strategic Superiority

In reality it was Franklin himself who was the founder of American intelligence, who understood true "Strategic Intelligence," which must be understood as going beyond the disposition and intentions of enemy forces and delve much deeper into the societies and very minds of both adversaries and allies alike.

It is a peculiar book. Daigler, as a retired CIA officer, examines revolutionary war intelligence with the skills he learned in his professional career, and therein lies a fundamental failing in this otherwise informative

John Paul Jones

Benjamin Franklin

history. However it is not his personal failing, but instead the failing of our intelligence services introduced during the Vietnam War.

This is seen very clearly in the nomenclature used throughout the book. Here the American Revolution becomes a rebellion for independence. This is a totally false understanding of the revolution and represents an intelligence failure of the highest order. There is nothing really "revolutionary" in a fight for independence. The American Civil War saw the southern states fighting for "independence" in order to perpetuate slavery, in effect renouncing the founding principles of our republic.

Our revolution was not a fight for "independence from the motherland" because of "taxation without representation." It was a fight for the creation of humanity's first republic, dedicated to the principle that "all men are created equal" and share the inalienable right to "life, liberty and the pursuit of happiness," where each individual's creative potential may best be realized. It was a fight of ideas. These were not conceptions restricted to the colonies, but were fundamental ideas that were sweeping through political, intellectual, and artistic currents throughout western civilization of the time. Therefore the American Revolution was the vanguard and front line of that struggle of ideas and the principles that set man above the beast.

The Enemy

The enemy was not the people of Great Britain or of Hessen, Germany, but the system of oligarchy premised on the proposition of "life, liberty and property," where property could include human beings then known as "subjects," or an overlordship, known as imperialism, over entire nations.

Franklin is received at the French Court, 1778.

While Washington led the fight across the battlefields of the territory of the united colonies, Franklin waged it in the heart of the beast and on both fronts. Franklin and Washington's most powerful weapons were ideas. Nowhere is this more evident than the struggle waged by Franklin. Revisionist history might tell us that Franklin deployed to Paris on the premise that the "enemy of my enemy is my friend" and saw his mission as persuading the French government, a monarchy as oligarchical as that of the British Crown, to support the American revolution through skillful manipulation, in order to acquire the rifles and cannons, and ultimately a powerful military ally, which would enable the defeat of the British on the field of battle. If he had accepted those limitations, Franklin would have failed miserably.

Franklin was the leading intellect of his era; a fact appreciated by all the leading statesmen, intellectuals, and scientists throughout all of Europe, including Great Britain itself of the time. Moreover, many of these men and women not only shared his political views but were active within the highest political circles, including the royal courts of their countries. This was particularly the case in France, Prussia, and Russia, in which efforts were being made to reform these monarchies. While these monarchies would render support to the American cause against Britain, they also knew they were playing with fire, a fact of which Franklin was very much aware. Once America gained independence, they knew no king would be invited, or imposed, to rule over the American people, and a state would be erected diametrically opposed to the concept of monarchy, or more specifically, oligarchy.

Daigler has an interesting insight, stating, "Perhaps the greatest irony in the intelligence history of the war is that while British intelligence activities were highly successful in collecting information regarding American-French plans and intentions in both a timely and comprehensive manner, British failure to use this information effectively in its policy formation and implementation negated most of its value."

This is one of the most important insights the author expresses in the entire book, but that same author does not elaborate on the observation, which should, in fact, serve as the beginning of an intelligence investigation.

Franklin, without doubt, knew that those in power in Britain would fail to make effective use of their intelligence in their policy formation, and that knowledge was a true piece of "strategic intelligence" for Franklin and the American cause.

Franklin knew that despite sympathy for the American cause within important circles in Britain, those in power were fully committed to an imperialist policy that left no room for compromise. The colonists, even if they were the "children" of the "mother country," could not be treated better than the Indians, Malays, or Africans suffering under the oppression of the East India Company.

While Washington can be correctly identified as founding the first military intelligence organization and being America's first practitioner of military intelligence, the true founder of American intelligence is Franklin himself. While there are many biographies and histories of Franklin's role in the revolution, the book written from an intelligence point of view has yet to be written.

China Goes Global with Ultra High Voltage Power Transmission

by Mike Billington

Aug. 26—China has made itself the world leader in ultra high voltage (UHV) electric power transmission, and is now taking this critical technology global, starting with a 2,000 km UHV line now being constructed in Brazil. State Grid Corporation of China and Electrobras of Brazil have now completed construction of the 11,233 MW Belo Monte Dam, the fourth largest hydroelectric dam in the world, on the Xingu River, a tributary of the Amazon. The power will be transmitted via the UHV line to the densely populated area of Rio de Janeiro.

Xinhua/Zhou Haijun

A technician examines a span of China's 759 km Huainan-Nanjing-Shanghai ultra high voltage transmission line.

UHV transmission is crucial, especially in larger countries, where electrical power is now transmitted at lower voltages across great distances. The higher voltage means the reduction of current (amperage) proportionately, and thereby lowers the loss of energy (as heat in the conducting transmission lines). Energy loss is a huge expense to a country, often due to inefficient systems (Haiti suffers nearly 60% loss), or due to the necessity of long transmission lines in large countries like Brazil, which suffers a 16% loss. The new UHV line in Brazil will reduce the loss to 7%.

The United States has one of the lowest loss rates in the world, at 6%, primarily due to the density of high output nuclear and other power plants in highly populated areas. Nonetheless, former U.S. Secretary of Energy Stephen Chu has called China's development of UHV technology a "Sputnik moment" for the United States, the *Financial Times* reported on June 6, 2018. "China has the best transmission lines in terms of the

highest voltage and lowest loss," Chu stated. "They can transmit electricity over 2,000 km and lose only 7% of the energy. If we transmitted over 200 km we would lose more than that."

China's Ambassador to Brazil, Li Jinzhang, told *People's Daily* that China's UHV technology is "a calling card of 'Made in China'.... This is the first time that China applies UHV technology abroad. Its construction inaugurates a new historic stage, which marks the recognition by other countries of UHV technology and other technologies created in China. Through the Belo Monte project, Brazil's government, businesses and local population expressed the will and interest in deepening mutually beneficial cooperation which is advantageous to all."

In fact, most functioning UHV lines active today are

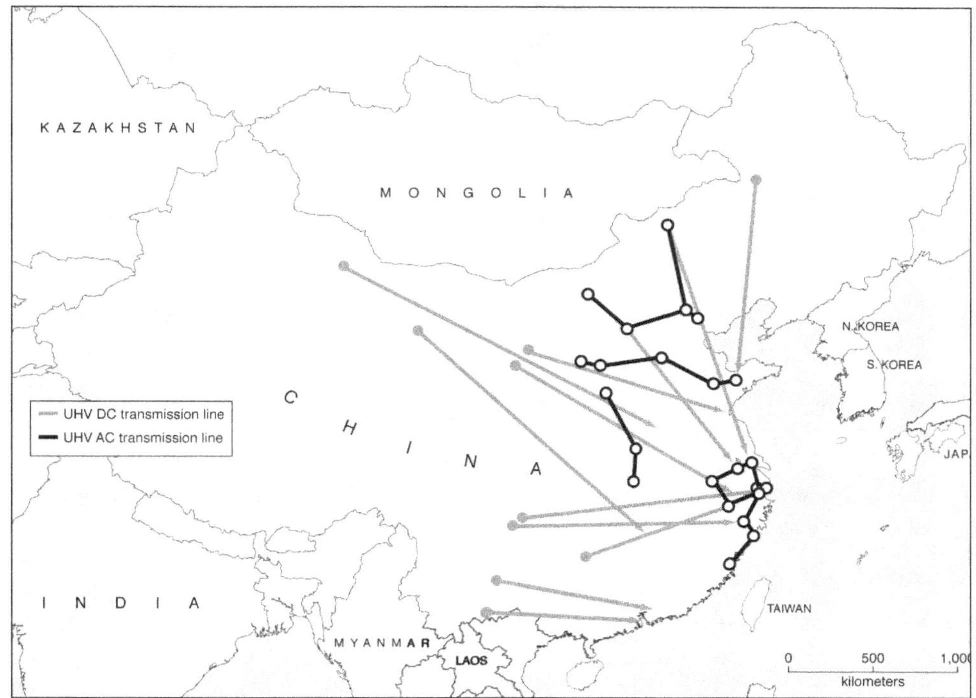

China's UHV electrical transmission lines. The longer blue lines are direct current (DC) with only a single destination, while the shorter black lines are alternating current (AC), which lose more energy but are capable of dispensing energy to several locations.

sian, Japanese and Korean power companies, to move power generated in Siberia to Seoul.

China Takes the Lead

China faces multiple problems which have necessitated the development of UHV transmission. The primary sources of hydroelectric power are in the northeast and the west, far from the large population concentrations along the eastern coast and the central provinces in the south. Huge coal deposits are also concentrated in these more distant regions. Coal can be moved, but the rail system has historically been overburdened by the movement of coal, while coal-fired electric power plants have been a major contributor to the serious air pollution conditions in the major Chinese cities. Producing the electricity near the coal mines and moving the energy efficiently via UHV lines will help resolve these problems.

Since 2006, China has built 19 UHV lines at a cost of billions of dollars, with a total length of over 30,000 km, supplying 4% of the national energy usage. Of the 19 lines, six are AC and 13 are DC, which is more efficient for very long distances. The AC lines are 1,000 kV, and the DC lines are 800 kV, although an 1,100 kV DC line is now under construction.

The 1,100 kV DC line will allow transmission over a distance as great as 5,000 km with a 12,000 MW capacity, suitable for international grids. The line now under construction will bring energy generated in Xinjiang Uygur Autonomous Region through five provinces—Gansu, Ningxia, Shaanxi, Henan and ending in Anhui—a total distance of 3,324 km. At completion—expected later this year—it will transmit 66 billion kilowatt-hours (kWh) of electricity every year. State Grid's website reports, "The ±1,100 kV Juggar East-Anhui South UHV Project is a first-class world UHV power transmission project with the highest voltage

in China, although there are plans to wheel electrical power generated from wind turbines in Oklahoma to Tennessee via a UHV line, and India is building UHV lines with Siemens technology. In Europe, the only UHV line connects the UK with France under the English Channel.

In 1980, the Soviet Union began construction of a 1,150 kilovolt (kV) alternating current UHV line in Kazakhstan, intended to move power from Kazakhstan to the industrial centers in the Urals. It was the largest UHV line in the world at that time. However, the UHV substations required were never constructed outside of Kazakhstan, so the transmission was reduced to 500 kV on the Russian side. After the demise of the Soviet Union, the entire system was downgraded to 500 kV.

China's State Grid, a state-owned company, runs nearly 90% of China's power grids, and is also building the UHV line in Brazil. State Grid is the second largest corporation in the world (behind Walmart) with just under $350 billion in revenues, according to the 2018 Fortune Global 500 list. The company plans to build an "Asian Supergrid" in cooperation with Rus-

The overhead 1,100 kV UHV power line under construction across the Yangtze River, April 2018.

for wind and solar, "since it was intermittent in nature and required the mixing of conventional electricity, like coal-fired plants, whose output was more stable throughout the day." One of the original UHV power lines, which had been intended to move wind- and solar-generated electricity from Xinjiang to Henan, is in maintenance half of the time "due to damage caused by huge load fluctuations."

On the other hand, just one of the UHV lines, the 1,680 km UHV DC, bringing power from the Xiloudu Dam in Yunnan Province to Zhejiang Province in East China, contributes 17% of Zhejiang's power during the summer, saving more than 30 million tons of coal and reducing air pollution dramatically.

China's innovation and world leadership in UHV power transmission—as in other areas of technology—is both transforming China at the most rapid pace of any nation in history, while also being made available throughout the world through the Belt and Road Initiative.

level, largest transmission capacity, longest transmission distance, and most advanced technology worldwide."

The original plan for the UHV grid projected 37 UHV lines by 2020, but this has been reduced due to the reduced demand from the time of the original estimates. According to *China Dialogue*, national demand growth averaged 11.7% from 2003 to 2012, but has fallen to 4.5% as of 2017.

China has invested heavily in wind and solar power facilities, which are also concentrated in the more distant regions of the west and northeast. As is the case with all of the solar and wind facilities promoted by the environmentalists, they are horribly inefficient and dependent on state subsidies. In the case of China, the UHV lines were intended in part to facilitate building these solar and wind farms in the distant areas, but these farms have proven unable to overcome the inherent limitations of these greenie-friendly power sources.

The *South China Morning Post* reported in 2016 that only 10-20% of the capacity of the UHV lines could be used

Technicians inspect an AC/DC converter station in Jinhua, Zhejiang province, June 23, 2017.

ZEPP-LAROUCHE WEBCAST

Time Has Come for a New Bretton Woods, Based on LaRouche's Four Laws

This is the edited transcript of the Schiller Institute's August 23, 2018 New Paradigm webcast, an interview with the founder of the Schiller Institutes, Helga Zepp-LaRouche. She was interviewed by Harley Schlanger. A video *of the webcast is available.*

Harley Schlanger: Hello I'm Harley Schlanger with the Schiller Institute. Welcome to this week's strategic webcast featuring our founder, Helga Zepp-La-Rouche.

Helga, the big news according to the "Get Trump" media and the anti-Trump fanatics was the dual events yesterday, the conviction of former Trump campaign chairman Paul Manafort on eight felony counts, and the plea bargain agreement, also of eight counts, of Trump's former attorney, Michael Cohen. Those media outlets are saying this is a slam dunk, that this is the end of Trump. LaRouche PAC put out a statement today, saying it's not true; it's not true at all. Trump's response was, there's still "no collusion," there's no crime.

I'd like to start with the status of Russia-gate now, in the aftermath of these two events. Where do things stand?

Russiagate Update

Helga Zepp-LaRouche: This is a very, very dangerous situation. The aim, as you said, is key here. There is absolutely no connection between what Manafort did before he became associated with the Trump campaign. What Michael Cohen is doing is highly dubious. The Federal judges, T.S. Ellis,— said that the whole purpose of this witch hunt is to terrorize Manafort or Michael Cohen in such a way that they, threat-ened with many years in jail, would turn against Trump and start "singing"—singing like canaries. The defendants, rather than reporting the truth, would start to "compose" just to get out of this. And this is obviously what Michael Cohen has done.

There is the payment to these women and the allegation that this is a campaign finance violation. Campaign finance violations happen in major campaigns all the time. Obama had to pay very large fines for violations. Former Presidential candidate John Edwards was accused of something similar and then was acquitted.

So this is all hyped up to proportions that bear no relation to Mueller's supposed mandate, which is ostensibly to prove that there was collusion between the Trump campaign and Putin and Russia. One might think that these two prosecutions, at this moment, are designed to increase the turnout of the Trump haters in

the upcoming midterm elections—to elect a Democratic majority to the Congress, at which point there would be enough forces to bring impeachment proceedings against Trump.

There is no substance to any of this. The ongoing investigations in the Congress into the collusion between the heads of the Intelligence services of the Obama Administration and British Intelligence, are not stopping. You have what is almost a countdown between these two processes. Look at the efforts by various British cabinet ministers coming to Washington, who are trying to reestablish the "special relationship" with the United States, which Trump had clearly cancelled, or basically put aside. The British are in an absolute frenzy against Russia and there is a growing frenzy against China, I think that that shows you what the real strategic intention of this is.

The good thing is that Trump, so far, has kept his nerve. However all kinds of foreign policy issues could go haywire. This is obviously an extremely dangerous situation.

What's an Honest and Moral Person To Do?

Schlanger: On the danger: there are now 75 days until the midterm elections, and there has to be a response, not just to the fraud of Russiagate, but to the underlying effort of Russiagate, which is to destroy Trump's potential, from changing the policy away from the Bush/Obama paradigm of confrontation and war, into a new paradigm of collaboration with Russia and China. What's being fought out over the next couple of months is not just a normal election, but what U.S. strategic policy will be, in relationship to Russia, to China; and what about the U.S. economy? There's so much to talk about here, but I'd like to begin with: What do people need to know about this strategic conjuncture, and what do they have to do?

Zepp-LaRouche: You have a worsening of the relationship between the United States and China. The Chinese are in the meantime absolutely convinced that the $16 billion in tariffs imposed on each side today, has nothing to do with trade as such, but everything to do with a futile attempt to curb the rise of China, and China's effort to become a world leader in certain high-tech areas by 2025. So this is no good. This is a terrible situation.

Almost every day new sanctions are being imposed on Russia. This also is absolutely terrible.

PIB of India

Indian Prime Minister Narendra Modi (left), Russian President Vladimir Putin (center), and Chinese President Xi Jinping (right) at SCO Summit.

There is now the danger of a near-term financial crash, much worse than that of 2008. The reverse carry-trade flow of capital—out of the emerging markets and into the dollar, into Wall Street, into the City of London—is a potential trigger for a collapse. Then you have many warnings that the "tapering" of the Federal Reserve must stop, that the Fed should go back to quantitative easing, full scale, because otherwise, there is the danger of a collapse way before the midterm elections.

So, if you look at all of these processes, the big question is, how can you address it all in such a way that you lift the discussion to a higher level? And that is why the Schiller Institute has put out a petition, calling for a New Bretton Woods conference, and especially appealing to the four leaders of the United States, Russia, China, and India—Trump, Putin, Xi Jinping, and Prime Minister Modi—to immediately agree to solve this problem and preempt a financial crash by going back to a Bretton Woods style fixed exchange rate regime, and establish a new international credit system in order to facilitate cooperation in the context of the New Paradigm, and the Belt and Road Initiative.

Now, is that realistic? I think it is. Russia, China,

and India are already very strongly cooperating along these lines. Trump has proven, in his initial relationships with China, and with his friendship with Xi Jinping, that he is absolutely capable of going in this direction. Trump's efforts to improve the U.S. relationship with Russia, especially his meeting with Putin in Helsinki, show that potential. The mad frenzy of the political establishment is at its core, a horrific fear of this potential.

We are right now collecting signatures from many people all over the world—and I appeal to everyone listening to sign the petition titled "The Leaders of the United States, Russia, China, and India Must Take Action." We want signatures from ordinary citizens and from leaders of institutions. We will soon publish an initial list of prominent signers. Many people from quite different walks of life—former military, former diplomats, people in high positions in different social organizations—who by signing have all agreed that the nations need to establish a higher level of cooperation if the world is not to go up in flames.

Also, please help by circulating our dossiers on the role of the British in this Russiagate affair. We have only a very short window of opportunity. Once a financial crash—an uncontrolled collapse—is underway, perhaps before the midterm elections, that crash could throw the world into irretrievable havoc and all kinds of crisis spots could go out of control. It is very urgent that we establish a higher level of cooperation of the major countries that do have the power to resist Wall Street and the City of London. The new discussion which came up, in this context, is a request from some people in Japan that we include Prime Minister Shinzo Abe and Japan into this list of countries. We are discussing this right now.

Let me underscore that that the Four Powers is not an exclusive club. The idea is to bring together a powerful enough combination, around which other countries will orient. We need a very solid initial powerbase in order to get this kind of reform. So, please, if you see reason in our proposal, sign the petition and distribute it to your friends and relatives and acquaintances and via social media. Help us build this movement for a New Bretton Woods. We have to change the agenda to prevent the world and its people from being destroyed by this complete frenzy and hysteria.

The 'Special Relationship' and Trident Juncture 2018

Schlanger: I think one of the points you just made, that people should take to heart, is that the hysteria of the reaction, to what we're doing, to what Trump is doing, is evidence that there is a fear among the geopoliticians, the neo-conservatives, and the anti-Trumpers, that we could succeed. Two or three months ago we issued a call to ditch the so-called "special relationship" of the United States with the British Empire, now we're now seeing one after another British official come before the U.S. Congress, to praise that "special relationship." This week it was Foreign Secretary Hunt, who in the discussions he had, kept saying: The "special relationship" is the core of the protection of the

C-SPAN
U.S. Assistant Secretary of State A. Wess Mitchell.

UN
UK Foreign Secretary Jeremy Hunt.

West against the aggressive Russians. Wess Mitchell, the person who replaced the discredited Victoria Nuland in the State Department, spoke in the Congress yesterday about the establishment of a new position called the Senior Advisor for Russian Malign Activities, who will coordinate anti-Russian activity with the British. So clearly, there's a reaction.

You were reporting earlier that there are plans for extended NATO maneuvers in October. What can you tell us about that?

Zepp-LaRouche: This is obviously a big provocation. Trident Juncture 2018, as it's called, may be the

German soldiers on maneuvers in Germany during Strong Europe Tank Challenge, May 8, 2017.

largest NATO military exercise since the end of the Second World War. It involves 40,000 soldiers from 30 countries, and will take place all along the Russian border, from Oct. 25 to Nov. 7, that is, until one day after the U.S. midterm elections. Later will come major Russian maneuvers.

When you have this kind of situation, military maneuvers can go very quickly from mere maneuver to hot war. I'm not saying that that is the plan, but in a world which is so unstable, where so many provocations are happening, where the tone is becoming so wild and so far out of proportion to what Russia has been doing, the risk of setting off actual war is high.

What is it that Russia and China are actually doing? Crimea was not annexed, and the lie that it was, is constantly being repeated up the wazoo. The coup against Ukraine was conducted—you mentioned Victoria Nuland—the State Department spent $5 billion on NGOs for a color revolution/regime change in Ukraine. There was the Maidan coup with a lot of Nazis involved. The vote of the people in Crimea [to reunify with Russia] was the reaction to all of these things. So it is not true that Putin annexed Crimea.

All the lies are repeated and repeated, and people generally have a very short memory for such things, this fake narrative becomes the "truth." That Germany will participate with 100 tanks in these maneuvers is really incredible. I know from many Russians that they are really very upset about the lack of gratitude from the German political class, for sure, because from the Russian agreement to a peaceful reunification of Germany in 1990, you would have expected that the promise made at the time not to extend NATO to the borders of Russia, would have been kept. But, no. Now, you have these war hawks joining in the provocations against Russia.

So this is terrible, and we have to absolutely counter that, reestablish diplomacy and dialogue as a means of solution to any problem, and not this kind of frenzy.

Schlanger: And we mustn't forget that one of the key actors in Ukraine on the U.S. side was former CIA Director John Brennan, who has been screeching and screaming because his role has been exposed, and he's out front. He's been so extreme that even some of his buddies, like James Clapper, are telling him to calm down a little bit.

In spite of all of the anti-Russian propaganda in the U.S. media, a Gallup poll yesterday said that 60% of Americans still favor better relations with Russia. This has been the policy that President Trump has called for from the beginning.

There was an initiative from the German Foreign Minister that seemed kind of strange to me. I wonder if you can enlighten us as to what Herr Maas is planning on doing.

What's German Foreign Minister Maas Up To?

Zepp-LaRouche: I'm not saying that it's not necessary for Germany to become more independent. The U.S. attempts to extend U.S. legislation all over the world doesn't have a democratic mandate. Therefore, there is an element of truth in what Heiko Maas

Former CIA Director John Brennan.

US-German relations: Foreign Minister Heiko Maas 'playing with fire'

As the US pursues an increasingly unilateral course, Heiko Maas has suggested forging alliances with nations favoring a multilateral world order. But Professor Thomas Jäger from Cologne University urges caution.

DW: German Foreign Minister Heiko Maas has suggested forging new international alliances. That

is saying, which is understandable and legitimate—that is that Germany should become more independent. That has, in fact, been our position for a very long time. What are Maas's solutions? He wants to have a German policy independent of the United States. He wants to militarize the European Union. When you look at the condition of the EU, you'll find that it all comes down to a Eurocentric "coalition of the willing," because there is no longer any EU unity, and not many countries in the EU intend to join the sharp anti-Russian tone of Maas, who has spoken out against both China and Russia.

The idea that you can build a Eurocentric independent Europe, with a payments system independent of the U.S. dollar, is not a bad idea, either, because no country wishes to be hit by U.S.-imposed secondary sanctions, sanctions with which it does not agree. However, I think it's an absolutely unworkable position. Why? A much broader conception is required, one that encompasses Eurasia from the Atlantic to the China Seas, from Vladivostok to Lisbon. A new economic union and a new security architecture are needed, not *against* the United States, but *including* the United States. You want to think in terms of getting a new system that works. Maas says the old partnerships don't exist anymore, which is true. The only partnership still functioning according to Maas, the one he wants to keep, is NATO. He wants to have an independent joint European military "intervention force," tasked with taking action in trouble spots all around the world.

I think that proposal is also a non-starter. It's bad because it's anti-Russia, it's anti-China, and it doesn't address the fundamental economic interests of Germany, which would be to cooperate with the projects of the New Silk Road in Africa and Southwest Asia. I think it is not a good thing.

Italy Launches Task Force China

Schlanger: While we're seeing chaos and disruption in the trans-Atlantic region, including in the United States, largely due to the idiocy of the Congress, we're seeing a continued, consistent drive from China to bring development to the world. There are a number of leading items of this that we can take up. I'd like to start with a development in Italy—the announcement by the Ministry for Economic Development of Task Force China, the main objective of which is to strengthen the relationship between Italy and China in many fields. How does that look, Helga?

Zepp-LaRouche: This is a very refreshing development. The new Italian Finance Minister, Giovanni Tria, is now heading a delegation in China. A second delegation now in China is being led by Michele Geraci, Italy's undersecretary of commerce. It was Geraci who announced the formation of Task Force China, with the idea to not just passively watch what is going on, but to keep pace with the shift of innovation and technology to Asia, and to China in particular. In a recent interview with *Corriere della Sera*, Geraci was asked if this is not China asserting untoward influence and other such usual questions. He said: No, China is the world leader in terms of infrastructure. Our infrastructure is in terrible condition (an obvious reference to the Morandi bridge that just collapsed in Genoa), and Chinese investment in Italian infrastructure is very welcome and needed. Geraci is also encouraging Italian firms not only to invest in China, but make joint ventures in all countries along the Eurasian Land-Bridge, and also in Africa. I think this is a very wonderful breath of fresh air.

As I mentioned already, more and more European countries want to cooperate with China: the new Austrian government, and the 16+1 Central and Eastern European countries (CEEC), Greece, Italy, Spain, Portugal. A trend for cooperation with China is clearly there.

In Germany, it is the Bavarians who are very happily talking about the extension of the New Silk Road into Bavaria. There have been a number of political exchanges between Bavarian and Chinese politicians and businessmen. I think that that is also a very good step in the right direction.

I don't know what will happen down the road. We are organizing to get *all* the European countries, and the United States, to cooperate with the New Paradigm. We need a lot of people to understand that mankind has reached a point where if we continue with geopolitical hysteria, the extinction of civilization could be very close. More people need to wake up and really understand that there is no reason why the major powers of this world cannot, or should not, cooperate in overcoming poverty, in overcoming underdevelopment. Go to Tennessee, or some of the southern states like Alabama or Mississippi. You'll find many pockets of people are living in Third World conditions. Germany, a so-called rich country, has 4.4 million poor children, and this is increasing! In Greece, the EU austerity policy has halved the funding for medical care, and 25,000 health-related jobs have been destroyed since the Troika began to ravage this country.

Now compare that to the absolutely impressive record of China, in which, as recently as 1978, some 97.8% of all people in rural areas were poor. In the last 40 years or 39 years, China has lifted 740 million people out of poverty. The total poverty rate in China today is only 3.1%. The Chinese government wants to reduce that percentage to zero, so that by 2020 there will be no poverty in China.

More people should cease being so hysterical, but instead look at the facts. Maybe China is doing something right, which the neo-liberal monetarist system is doing wrong. China is now offering its own model of economic transformation and sharing that experience, for example, with Africa. At the beginning of September, a very major conference will take place in Beijing, involving China and almost all African heads of state. Xi Jinping will keynote the conference and is expected to announce many new areas of cooperation between China and Africa—many areas of joint science, joint education, and other new things.

Two Incompatible Dynamics in the World

There are two dynamics: one is development and cooperation, and the other confrontation, which brings the danger of war. So people should really make up their minds on what side of history they want to be on. Be part of the Schiller Institute, become a member, sign our petition, and become active. Don't stand on the sidelines at the most crucial moment in history. If you are an American, you should make sure that this coup attempt against Trump is defeated. You don't have to agree with all of Trump's policies—that's not the point. The point is to defeat a coup that would bring back a crew of people who have become absolute war hawks, who, if in the driver's seat, will bring the world into absolute danger. Should those war hawks be returned to power, the potentials that now exist will be destroyed and probably could not be revived, and we would descend into a disaster of unprecedented historical dimensions.

Schlanger: You've just described what really should be an exciting challenge to all of our viewers—not merely the opportunity to defeat the evil that's represented by the people running Russiagate, but even more exciting, the potential in Africa with this conference coming up on Sept. 3 and 4 in Beijing. The New Silk Road Spirit is now infecting much of Central America—in El Salvador, in Mexico, in Panama. This is something which would be an obvious benefit to the United States, just as the development of Africa could stem the flood of refugees crossing the Mediterranean into Europe. The development of Honduras and El Salvador, parts of Mexico that were damaged by NAFTA, brings a tremendous opportunity. This is what the people running Russiagate are trying to stop, in order to keep us in the old paradigm.

Helga, I think you had some thoughts on El Salvador, as another example of a shift occurring worldwide?

Zepp-LaRouche: Yes. The U.S. State Department had a very negative reaction to it. El Salvador's new President, Sánchez Cerén, just delivered a nationally televised speech repeating his election campaign promise to transform the lives of all families in El Salvador, and that the new relationship with the People's Republic of China would be very beneficial in this direction.

There are more countries joining, realizing that being aligned with Taiwan and not accepting the One-China policy will not bring them any advantages. The way to go is with the New Silk Road.

Similar things are happening all over Ibero America, in which there are several horrible crisis situations

Creative Commons

Salvadoran President, Salvador Sánchez Céren, in 2017.

right now. In Argentina and Brazil we see very wild situations. In Argentina, they're ganging up against former President Christina Fernández de Kirchner. The question, really, is what is the directionality that brings cohesion, which brings peace, which brings a future? I think that more and more countries want a future—it's that simple.

We are in a time of enormous upheaval. There are two dynamics at play.

One is to keep the oligarchical system of neo-liberalism that expanded like cancer after President Richard Nixon decoupled the dollar from gold in 1971, and got rid of the fixed exchange rates. There are people who just want to keep that system which only benefits a very few, which is really the reason why all these wars of intervention took place. Remember, at the time of the second Gulf War, George Bush, Sr. said that the United States had to go in there to "protect the American way of life." Well, I think that that is an untenable position.

The big question now is can China's approach succeed? It is a new model of superpower cooperation, based on sovereignty and on respect for other nations' social systems, with win-win cooperation of all nations. Or, is the confrontation going to cause what some have called the "Thucydides trap," referring to the tensions preceding the

Peloponnesian War between Sparta and Athens, which led to the demise of ancient Greece—will that be repeated? Now, with nuclear powers, this could be the end of humanity.

Study the New Paradigm, Sign Our Four Power Petition

People should really study the New Paradigm, help the Schiller Institute bring some reason into the debate and show the options which exist for change.

Let me repeat my appeal to you: Sign our petition for a Four Power Agreement, get it around to all the people you know. Join our mobilization to bring in a completely different level of discussion and debate, a level of reason among all nations in order to protect world peace and bring in development. Let us look toward the future. Let us deepen our understanding of what humanity is all about. We are not animals. We don't go around killing each other for

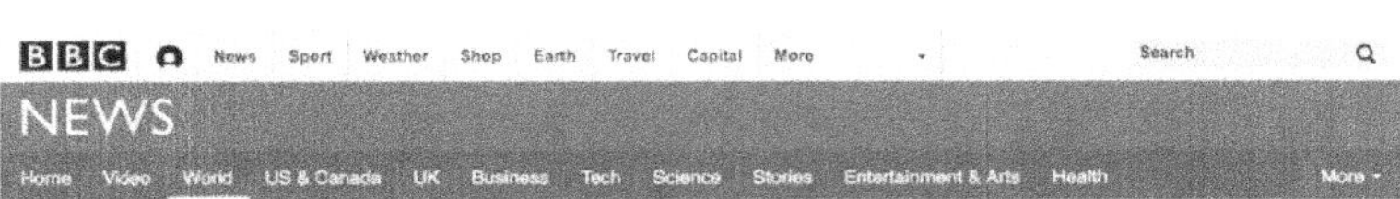

no other purpose than to fill our stomachs like wild animals tend to do. We are a species of reason, we can discover the laws of the universe, we can have space exploration, we can make new scientific discoveries. We can have a completely different identity as human beings, relating to each other as scientists, composers, and poets.

For mankind to survive, we have to make this qualitative jump to a new cultural renaissance. If we cling to this old, geopolitical paradigm, our future will be even more grim. So, join our efforts and become a member! Help us to circulate this petition and get as many signatures as possible.

Schlanger: Helga, you just summarized the exciting challenge before all of us, to truly become human. The Schiller Institute has just published a new report, *The New Silk Road Becomes the World Land-Bridge: A Shared Future for Humanity, Vol. II* Everyone who doesn't already have a copy of this report should go to our site and purchase one, so you yourself become familiar in detail with these ideas we have been speaking about in these webcasts, as well as the detailed Belt and Road projects around the world. There, you will learn more about China's new model for economic development and what we are calling the New Paradigm.

Is there anything else you wish to add, Helga?

Zepp-LaRouche: I want to encourage all of you to go to the archives of the various LaRouche associated websites—for example that of the Schiller Institute, the LaRouche PAC and the *EIR* website, as well as all of our other websites internationally—and read (or re-read) all the writings of my husband. He has addressed all of these issues in the most profound way, and his scientific method is more urgently needed today than at any time before. Become familiar with these ideas. There is a lot of unclarity about a lot of these issues, so, I urge you to study Lyndon LaRouche.

Schlanger: Good advice. OK, Helga, we'll see you next week.

Zepp-LaRouche: OK, hopefully in cooler weather.

Lyndon LaRouche Calls on the U.S., China, Russia and India To Create A New Bretton Woods System

The following is an edited transcript of the Saturday, August 18, 2018 LaRouche PAC Manhattan Project Dialogue with Dennis Small, including Small's presentation and key excerpts from Lyndon LaRouche's seminal November 18, 2008 webcast.

Dennis Speed: Today, we will begin with a video clip from Lyndon LaRouche, speaking on November 18, 2008, in the LaRouche PAC national webcast The full transcript is posted here: https://www.larouchepub.com/lar/2008/webcasts/3547nov18_opener.html

Lyndon LaRouche: What we're involved in today, is a general breakdown crisis of the world financial-monetary system. There is no possible rescue of this system, as such: that is, the present, international monetary system cannot be rescued. If you try to rescue it, you will lose the planet. You have to choose: Replace the system, or get a new planet....

There's no way that you can reorganize under the present world monetary-financial system. You have to put the whole system into bankruptcy reorganization.

Now, how can you do that? Well, what you can do, is end the existence of monetary systems: You put them into bankruptcy and close them out. Well, what do you do for money? We go back to the U.S. dollar. Our Constitution is unique among nations, in many respects....

So, what we can do, is, very simply, is we can go back to the U.S. Federal Constitution, and create what's called a "credit-based dollar," as opposed to a "monetary dollar." A credit-based dollar is consistent with our Constitution: that no money, as legal currency, as legal tender, can be uttered under the U.S. Constitution, without a vote by the U.S. Congress on behalf of action by the U.S. Presidency.

A Credit Based Dollar

So, in our system, the official currency of the United States, insofar as we follow our own Constitution, is limited to dollars, or dollar-equivalent negotiables, which are uttered *only* by previous authorization of the U.S. Congress, especially the House of Representa-

EIRNS/Stuart Lewis

Lyndon LaRouche

tives, and uttered by the U.S. Federal government! There is no such thing as an international monetary source, which gives us our currency—not legally. It is uttered by the U.S. government; it is sovereign. We are a sovereign state, and our currency is uttered by us, under our Constitution: by approval of the House of Representatives, and by the Presidency. No other currency exists.

In Europe, that is not the case: In Europe, the monetary systems are not controlled by the government.

They are created by central banking systems, which may negotiate with governments, and have agreements with governments, but the governments do not control the monetary system, as such. In point of fact, that is the *essence* of a free-trade system: that the governments have no essential control, as issuing authorities, over debt and credit outstanding.

And it's because of the utilization of that provision, that artificial money was created, by people making a capital promise, in capital amount, to go into debt, to get a lesser amount of money uttered in their behalf, now. That's how the world incurred a presently outstanding debt, through such means as derivatives, in the order of *quadrillions of dollars!*, far in advance of anything that could ever be paid. So, we are *never, never going to pay those debts!* We *couldn't* pay those debts. So, we're never going to pay them.

What Kind of Bankruptcy?

What do you do in a case like that? What does the United States do in a case like that, under our Constitution? You declare those debts *in bankruptcy*. And what do you do with them in bankruptcy? You sort them out! Those things that should be supported, will be supported, and the rest of it will just wait, or die away. The great majority, the vast majority of the obligations outstanding today, as nominal claims against countries, *will be cancelled*. Those things which should be paid, will be paid. Those otherwise, will never be paid. And they will never be paid, in any case!

Now, you have two ways to go: Either you collapse the world, with starvation and mass death, and those effects. Or, you put the thing through *bankruptcy reorganization*. And how do you do that? Well, what I specified is very elementary: I have four nations in mind that can take the lead on this thing. And the four nations, which together, represent the greatest consolidation of power on this planet: These nations are the United States, Russia, China, and India, as joined by other nations, which join in the same deal. We put the world through bankruptcy reorganization. How do we do it? We use the U.S. Constitution to do that.

The U.S. Constitution is unique in the fact we have a kind of Federal Constitution we have: that our dollar is not a monetary dollar; it's a credit dollar. In other words, the United States has uttered an obligation, on behalf of the U.S. government, which can be monetized. That is our obligation; that's our only obligation, and any other kind of obligation is not fungible.

Other countries have a different kind of system.

Four Major Powers Can Create a New System

Now, if the United States says, that we are going to back up our dollar, and enters into an agreement with Russia, China, and India, to join us, with other countries, in doing the same thing, to put the world through bankruptcy reorganization, in which we will *cancel* most of the outstanding financial obligations: It has to happen. Otherwise, no planet! If you try to collect on quadrillions of dollars of outstanding claims, from whom are you going to collect, by what means, and what's the effect? It is *against natural law*, to collect on that debt! How many people are you going to kill, to collect that debt? How many countries are you going to destroy, to collect that debt?

So, we have this monetary authority outside, which has treaty agreements with governments, but which has no real obligation to governments otherwise, except the treaty agreement. This agreement has resulted in the creation of a vast world debt, a monetary debt, which can never be paid. Well, obviously, the system is bankrupt! You shut down the system, and put it into bankruptcy reorganization—it's the only remedy.

How does it work for us? Under our Constitution, any credit we utter, in a monetizable form, is an obligation under the authority of the U.S. government, in each process, by the approval of the Congress, the uttering of it, and by the action of the Federal government, with that approval. Now, also, not only do we utter our currency, properly, under those terms, but if we, as a nation, as a sovereign republic, enter into an agreement, a treaty agreement with other countries, for the same system, then under the treaty agreement, other countries enjoy the advantage of the same system we have for reorganization of our debts.

And that's the only way we can get out of this mess.

So, we create a group of nations, who are operating under treaty relationship with the United States, which gives Constitutional protection to this, so that we now have created a new system—a credit system—to replace the existing monetary system. And everything that is put under the protection of the *credit system*, is now solid. Everything else is thrown onto the floor, to see what you can pick up: It's in bankruptcy.

So therefore, we can create a new credit system, among nations, which I think—if the United States,

Russia, China, and India agree, most nations of the world will happily join us, especially considering the alternative. And therefore, we can create a new world system, a new money system, a credit system as opposed to a monetary system. And under those conditions, we can proceed to advance credit on a large scale, for physical reconstruction of the world's physical economy. We can organize a recovery of the same type, which we undertook with President Franklin Roosevelt, back in the 1930s and 1940s. And we won't change from that, I should think, once we've done it.

That's the only alternative.

A New System Means the End of British Empire Looting

Now, what that means is, politically, the end of the British Empire; or what's called the British Empire. The British Empire is the present world empire. There is no other empire on this planet today, except the British Empire. The use of the "empire" to describe any other system, is incompetent. The British are the only empire, and the British Empire is that which controls the dollar, the floating dollar today, the monetary dollar.

So, under these conditions, we then proceed to world reconstruction. And what we do, instead of the present free-trade system, is we go back to a protectionist system, a fixed-rate system; in other words, currencies will have a fixed rate of exchange with respect to each other, or adjustable by treaty arrangements, but they do not float. And we then proceed to utter the credit, for large-scale infrastructure investment, which will be the driver of the physical reconstruction of the planet. *That's the only remedy.* Any suggestion but that, is insane. Any failure to do exactly what I've prescribed, is insane. All sane people will, therefore, immediately agree—or we will have to draw the obvious conclusion.

So, that's what I outlined, in essence, as to how this would work—that's the core of it. This is the U.S. Constitution. It's a system which worked, every time we've used it. If we go back to it once again, as we did under Franklin Roosevelt, we'll come out of this nicely....

And our remedy is to use great power on this planet, to force through a system, a fixed-exchange-rate system, to establish a credit system in place of a monetary system, and to launch large-scale projects through joint credit structures which finance these projects, which enable nations to build their way out of the present physical mess we have today.

It's a tough one. And people say, "Why do you want to do that? Couldn't you take *slo-o-w-er* steps? Slo-o-wer steps?" "Well, you know that train's coming down the track, and you're walking across it—do you think you should take slo-o-wer steps?"

No. So therefore, what you need, is you need these four countries. And they are different countries, as you may have noticed, not only different as nations, but they have different characteristics. We have one characteristic, as the United States, when we're functioning properly. Russia has certain characteristics which are unique to Russia. China has characteristics, including social characteristics, which are unique to China. India has characteristics which are different than any of the other countries. But this is a great part of the human race, the population, totally.

And you have countries that are associated with them, like Japan. Japan's market is principally Asia. Its best market, for its high-tech production, are neighboring countries of Asia, which include Siberia, include the mainland of China, and so forth—that region of the world. Japan has a high-technology capability, which is extremely valuable. Korea—especially South Korea, but really Korea as a whole—has also a very significant potential. Also Korea is different than Japan and China, and Russia, and therefore Korea is a very valuable country, in the sense that it's not the same as China, Japan, Russia, and so forth.

And therefore, the cooperation among these countries of different characteristics is a very important stabilizing factor in the world situation. It also is a key part in production. India has completely different characteristics in this respect, but it also has, in effect, similar problems. The most common problem, is power. Now, we have nuclear power, developed today. It's the only

The four powers.

decent power, that we have for dealing with these kinds of problems....

A System That Respects and Develops All Human Life

What we need in the United States, and other parts of the world, is the basic development of improved infrastructure, as it affects human life and production, in order to increase the productive powers of labor per capita. That's what we need in the United States. We need to increase the productive powers of labor.

At the same time, we have a population, which, over the past period, over the past 40 years!—40 years! *Forty years!*—the United States has been losing productivity per capita over 40 years. It started back in 1967-1968, we began to lose, shrink, net infrastructure development: Over the course of time, we lost our industry, we lost our productivity, we lost science, we have people doing kinds of work that is not work any more, just make-work to keep them busy; and services, to service services, to service services. We destroyed that! We have a people that no longer have the *skills* to produce what they used to be able to produce with the same population then, today. We've lost that.

We have been insane *for 40 years!* Since 1967-68, Fiscal Year '67-68. We have been losing infrastructure.... We destroyed essential parts of the productivity of the entire planet; we destroyed technology, with these measures.

And therefore, we have great needs for breakthroughs in technology, which are within our reach; but we also have to be able to assimilate technology, by what? By improving infrastructure: the infrastructure which is necessary to enable labor of a certain skill to improve its productivity, because we have unskilled people! We don't have the skilled labor population we had 40 years ago! We've lost it! We have a very small fraction of that. We're about to lose much more of that, right now....

Skilled Labor and Infrastructure

Therefore, if you look at this, look at the process by which we have been destroyed from what we were becoming, and had become, up until the end of the last war, especially since 1968 to approximately '71. If you look at that, you see, this is not some "natural" process: This is the natural *consequence* of an intentional direction of policy in the wrong direction! ...

So, we're in trouble today, only because we made that change—and we've made it again, back in the same direction.

Now, the question is: Do we want to survive? If we want to survive, we have a lesson of how to survive, in what Roosevelt in particular accomplished as President, during the time he was President. We can survive. But, if we don't, we're not going to survive. As a matter of fact, with the present conditions, if those changes are not made, you must expect that there will never be a recovery of the economy: *This present crisis will be a permanent one....*

That's our situation now.

So therefore, that's what I laid out on Tuesday, last Tuesday. It's an outline of exactly the policy we can follow. If we can reach agreement, in the United States— I don't care who the current President, I don't care who the President-elect is. We have a Presidential *system* which is more important than any President: Can the *Presidential system* of the United States decide to reach an agreement with Russia, China, and India—*now!*—to take joint action, which will turn the planet around. And that joint action *would turn the planet around!*

Are we willing to do that? With the understanding that we're going back to the kind of policy that Franklin Roosevelt represented in his time, that we know we must represent, relative to our circumstances in our time? If we're willing to do that, and if we can engage Russia, China, and India, which are countries completely different in culture than our own, and different than each other; if we can engage in that, with those four nations, and others, to make a commitment to say, "This is not going to happen to us: We're going to take action to transform this planet. We're going to move upward," we can survive, we can succeed.

Are we willing to do that? If we are, we can survive. And if we're not, we're a bunch of fools! And richly deserve what's going to happen to us, if we're not willing to do that. That's the issue....

So that's our part—and some of us have to stand up, as I'm doing, and take leadership in this situation. Because, if we do it, we have in our hands the ability to introduce the policies that will succeed. If we bring together cooperation among the United States, Russia, China, and India, and other countries follow and join that, *we can turn this world situation around.* We can get back to something which is going in a different direction—we can do that. And the question today, is, are we willing to do that?

We Need a Morality of a Special Type

The problem today, is a question of morality of a special type: When I was younger—and when some of you, who are approximately my age, or verging upon it, were younger—when you thought about life, you generally thought about two generations of preceding generations, grandfather and father's generation; and you thought about two generations to come, you thought about becoming a grandfather, and the two generations that would come afterward. Many people who immigrated into the United States thought that way.

They came here as poor people, from poor countries, or poor conditions in other countries, and they looked forward to their children succeeding and their grandchildren succeeding. The idea of coming over to the United States, as a laborer, in New York City, and ending up with a grandchild as a scientist or a doctor or something. It was a sense of achievement and that was the mentality of people from that time, people coming to this country as a land of opportunity to become something, to develop into something.

That's not the standard today. The standard is much more selfish. Self-centered is, "When I stop breathing, I don't care any more." In my generation, or in older generations, that was not the standard. We said, "I'm going to stop breathing, but what I'm doing is going to go on. The process I'm part of, is going to go on." And therefore, you weren't a dog, you were a human being. And like a human being, you thought in terms of coming generations, as well as past generations; you thought of how you had come into being, you thought about your background, you tried to learn from your family's experience, and the experience around you of older generations; you tried to see where the country's going; you tried to see what role you were playing in the country; and thinking about raising a family, and seeing what comes of that family two or three generations from now.

And life was organized around this kind of idea, of family and community. Of a meaning of being somebody, and who you were in a community that's growing and evolving with successive generations, about four, five, six generations, was the context of your life.

Your Immortal Interest

And if you did a little study of history, you would look back further, a few hundred years; or if you studied as I did, you'd look back a few thousand years. And look ahead at least a couple hundred years. And you situated your life, in what your role is now, in the time-phase you occupy in life—relative to a few thousand years before you, and maybe a hundred or more years to come.

And that's where you located your interest! Your interest in *being*, was not what you experienced while you were alive. But what you experienced in knowing what you were part of, in times past and times to come! What you were determined to help *cause* to be the case, in times to come! It's like the grandfather who would take his grandson out to a large project, like the Tennessee Valley project of the old days, and saying to the grandson, "I helped build this. See what I helped build." And that was the standard of life.

The problem today, is that standard doesn't exist. It exists in rare people; it exists to some degree in a feeling and anticipation of desire; it's the desire to be human, the desire to have a sense of immortality. But there's not much substance to it. There's not much confidence in it, because the society doesn't encourage you to think in those terms.

And so that's the situation before us. We can solve this problem, and discuss it here. We can solve these problems: But we have to understand the problem. We have to understand that we are now at the end of civilization. That the policies which are being presented to us, by high-level sources in the United States, in Europe generally, lead to an absolute disaster for humanity in the very near term.

There is no question whether this system is coming down or not! It is coming down, now! And without the kind of radical changes that I indicate, this system is coming down this year! This year and the coming year. It's coming down: It's gone! There's nowhere else to run to! You want to live in Hell? Stay where you are. No need to change, no need to travel: Just stay where you are, it'll come to you.

Do You Have the Guts to Risk Changing?

But, the point is: Are you willing to take the risk of changing? Are you willing to fight the war that has to be fought, rather than some war you would rather fight? That's the situation today. That's my situation. You've got to think in those terms. I've spelled this out in writing, I've spelled it out in the past weeks' time, in several ways, in a number of pieces. The situation is clear to me, we can win; it's possible. But, it's not likely, is it? You have to make it likely. Maybe some of us have the guts to do it.

Dennis Small: You just heard the keynote address of the day. It's remarkable how Lyndon LaRouche's comments from a decade ago are absolutely applicable to the situation we're immediately facing; both in terms of the diagnosis of the problem, as well as most emphatically the proposed solution. The immediate 80- or 90-day period ahead is one that actually is only understood from the standpoint of the perspective which Lyndon LaRouche just laid out for us. We are facing an imminent collapse of the entire trans-Atlantic system. We're facing an attempted coup d'état against President Donald Trump, in which the upcoming elections in November are absolutely critical. We have to awaken the American population to make sure that that coup d'état does not actually transpire.

At the same time, there is the ongoing activity of those who are putting together a global alternative to this catastrophe. On September 3-4, there will be a major diplomatic event of the Forum on China-Africa Cooperation (FOCAC). The nations of Africa will be meeting with China to discuss the policy of development which is applicable not simply to Africa, but to the entire planet under the Belt and Road Initiative. We have also in September, from the 11th to the 13th, the meeting of the Eastern Economic Forum in Vladivostok, Russia, which is an occasion where not only Russia and China will be getting together—two of the Four Powers which Lyn has talked about—but many other nations as well. We trust that there will be a high-level American delegation there as well.

Then, a little bit later in November, we have this meeting in Shanghai, China of the International Expo, an import expo by the Chinese. Most countries hold export fairs of what they want to export to the world; not China. They have a fair of what they want to import from every nation in the world as part of their global industrial and infrastructure thrust around the Belt and Road Initiative. So, we're looking at a period where everything that was unleashed almost 50 years ago today, on August 15, 1971, is now coming to a head.

Fixed Exchange Rates Not About Money

Let's just go back 47 years to what happened in August 1971. As we've discussed, this was the declaration by Nixon that the dollar was being taken off the gold standard and that the fixed exchange rate system

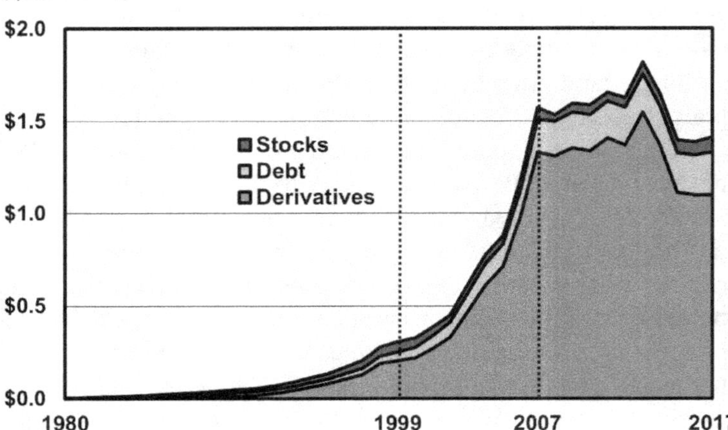

was over. A system of floating rates was established, which basically allowed massive speculation in a new currency that was created at that time. It was called the dollar, but it's not the U.S. dollar; it's the London-based speculative dollar, which is a different currency than the U.S. national dollar, which should be issued through a national bank as per Hamilton.

So, that separation occurred, which allowed for massive speculative activity to occur and a new situation was created, because there were no longer fixed exchange rates and there was free convertibility with no exchange controls. For Third World countries and other countries that need to convert their currencies into dollars, what it meant was that their currency, like our dollar, was separated from and became different from the actual U.S. national dollar basis of the Bretton Woods system. August 1971 was the beginning of the end of the Glass-Steagall system. First as it expressed itself in the relationship to Third World countries, and then shortly thereafter, in 1999, with the formal revocation of the Glass-Steagall bill, inside the United States.

Nixon Pulled Plug on FDR's Bretton Woods

Now what this did, as you're undoubtedly aware, is that it unleashed an absolutely enormous firestorm of speculative activity. What you see on the screen now is a graph [**Fig. 1**], "World Financial Aggregates" in which we used the actual numbers in the growth of the world's financial aggregates. The first vertical line is 1999. You can see that after the end of Glass-Steagall in

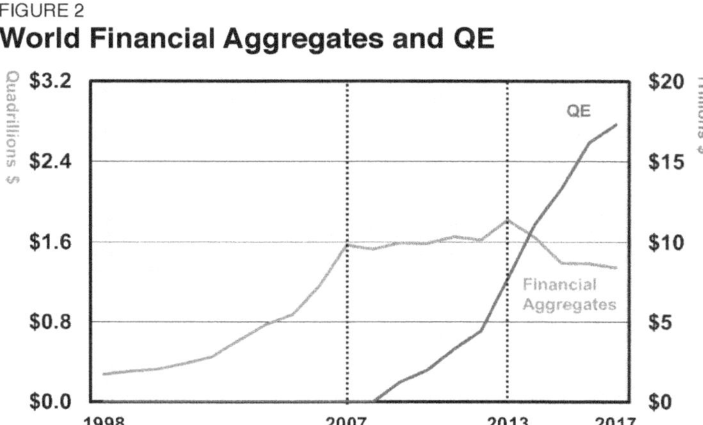

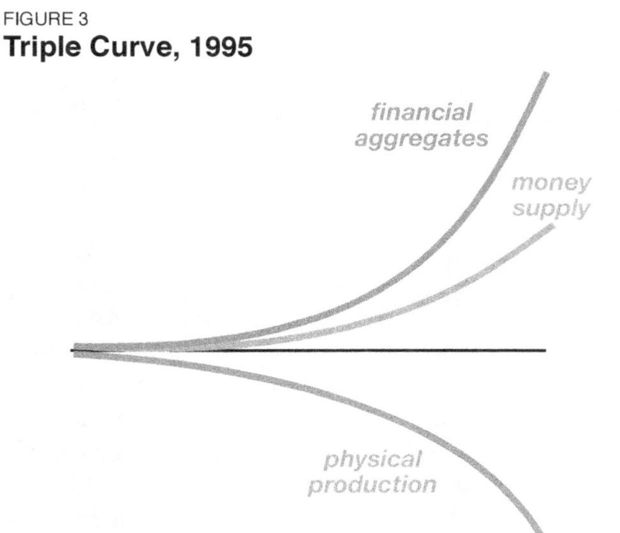

the United States, this bubble took off. This is a cancer. The lion's share of it was then, and still is today, derivatives; it's not debt, it's not the stock market, as bad as those are. It's derivatives, which are essentially bets on bets on bets, based on absolutely no real physical production whatsoever. It's sort of like what LaRouche was just talking about, services to service, to services, which service services. Derivatives are the equivalent of that in the financial world.

Now, you'll notice that this grew astronomically, exponentially, from 1999 to 2007; that's the point where the crisis, the meltdown of 2008, begins and occurs, which is the point at which LaRouche is addressing the crisis.

And what you have is a period of relative stagnation of the growth of that financial bubble, followed in the period of around 2013-2014 by a significant drop in global financial derivatives. Back up in the peak here of about $1.8 quadrillion is when we were saying this thing is heading to $2 quadrillion and then some. It has since dropped back down. This is not good: this is bad, the way this has occurred.

Because this has happened, as you can see in this next graph [**Fig. 2**], "World Financial Aggregates and QE," despite the fact, or perhaps because of the fact that during this same period, as the financial aggregates were rising, in 2008 the famous policy of "quantitative easing" began— the policy of "funny money" or "let's feed the cancer, boys." We have had a growth of quantitative easing of monetary aggregates under quantitative easing. This is measured on a different axis than the derivatives, which is the first Y axis.

You get the idea of the trend here which is what I want to show. You're talking about $18 trillion in quantitative easing, whose purpose originally, as you can see here, was designed to bolster the overall cancerous bubble of the financial aggregates, but was insufficient to do so. It accelerated and not only was it insufficient to do so, but actually the financial aggregates began to collapse.

Incredible Stupidity of Quantitative Easing

Now what is happening? You may have heard of the famous discussion, "Well, let's 'taper' the quantitative easing: Let's raise interest rates, let's slow down the rate of increase of quantitative easing," which some of the bankers are talking about, because they see where this is heading for a total blowout. If you look at the top of this quantitative easing curve, you can see that it is "tapering," under conditions where an astronomical increase, a geometric increase of the quantitative easing was insufficient to keep the financial bubble going. What do you think is going to happen, if and when this tapering actually continues? It's going to blow sky high. This is why you have even some bankers saying "this thing is going to blow up." It could very well blow up in the United States before the November elections.

How did LaRouche foresee these kinds of developments? He certainly didn't have a crystal ball to predict the specific numbers, but you didn't need that. The specific numbers are frankly somewhat irrelevant. What he had was a method of analysis which people will be familiar with as his famous [**Fig. 3**] "Triple Curve or Typical Collapse Function," in its first iteration in Novem-

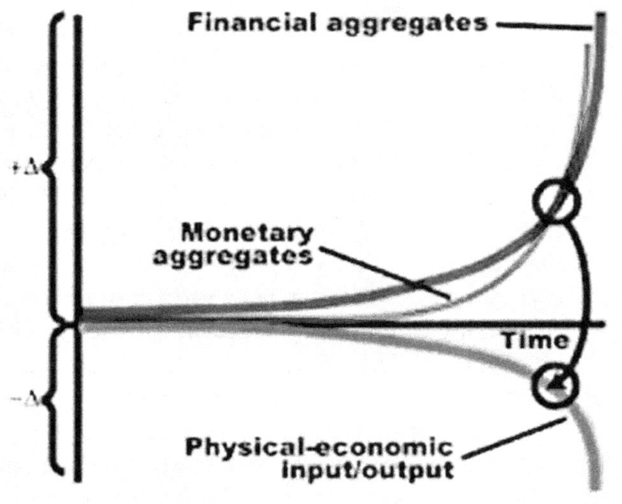

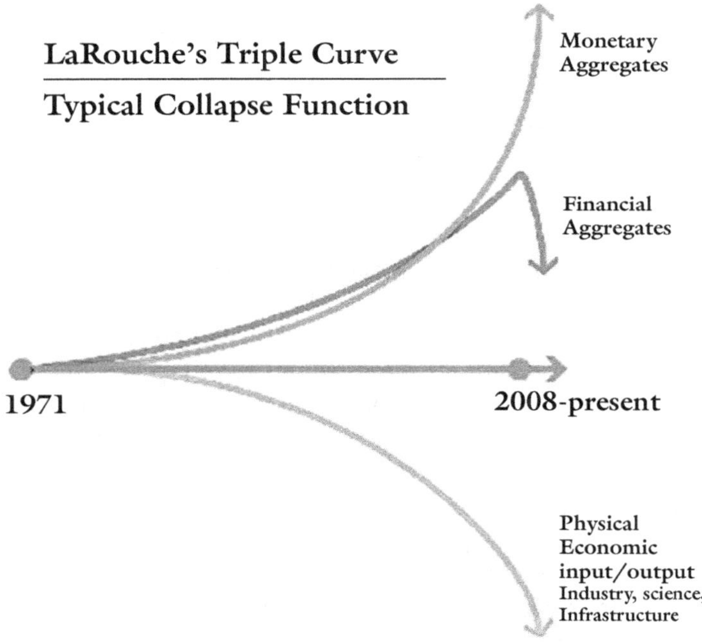

ally collapsing as measured in potential relative population-density.

This is where we were around 1996—so far so good, or actually, so far so bad. This was our real financial-economic condition after the 1971 destruction of the Bretton Woods system.

LaRouche's Triple Curve

Later, LaRouche produced this next iteration [**Fig. 4**], "The Collapse Reaches a Critical Point of Instability," of the same basic concept. He said, this is what happens when the collapse reaches a critical point of instability. What you have, is a point where the rate of increase of monetary aggregates—the green line—is greater than the rate of increase of financial aggregates (in red). In other words, to be able to allow the cancer to keep growing at the rate at which cancers grow, you have to increase your monetary aggregates, such as quantitative easing, even more rapidly.

Now, that really does not work. And in fact what happened, which you can see in this 2008 iteration of the triple curve [**Fig. 5**]. This was just about the time, or a little bit later than LaRouche's November 18, 2008 webcast (with which we started). He said then that after you've reached this point of critical instability, no matter how rapidly you raise your monetary aggregates, the financial aggregates cannot be maintained. It's going to blow out, period. The Tulip Bubble blows up.

This 2008 graphic is where we stand today, at exactly that point. Keep this graphic in mind, and look back at Figure 2, "World Financial Aggregates and QE," again. Now again, these are different absolute values and different scales, but you can see what is actually going on here. Despite the rate of increase of monetary aggregates, as represented in quantitative easing, the financial aggregates are collapsing.

Where is this going? This is heading straight to Hell. Exactly when? That much is an open question for sure, but it's not far from now, and it's something that cannot be avoided inside this system.

The critical point in all of this is the bottom curve—the physical aggregates, the physical economic system; that's the real problem. Who cares what happens with monetary aggregates or derivatives. The problem, as LaRouche just explained in this video, is that the attempt to defend and save the cancer means a policy of

ber 1995. You can see the money supply (in green) growing; the financial aggregates (in red) growing above the money supply curve, at a more rapid rate. The Y axis here is not an absolute amount; it is the rate of growth. The collapse of physical production (in blue) has to underlie any functional economy if that economy is going to survive, but that production has been actu-

genocide. It means destroying the population, by reduction of living standard, by reducing the technological level, by making it impossible to have a growing potential relative population-density to match the growth of the actual population.

Potential Relative Population-Density Destroyed

Now, what happens when your potential relative population-density is *less* than your actual population? People die! There's wars, there's drugs all over the place, there's opioid epidemics; there's mass migration if you happen to be a Third World country. If you want to know what's actually behind the crisis of migration and drugs, look at it from the standpoint of potential relative population density.

Look at what has happened cumulatively, as of 2015, in terms of emigration to the United States from Mexico and Central America. Today it's even worse. Look at Mexico: With a total population of about 126 million, of those born in Mexico, i.e., first-generation Mexicans, 11.5 million have migrated to the United States—that's 9.1% of the population. It is the same in Guatemala and Honduras. El Salvador is the extreme case: A fifth of the population has migrated to the United States. It is the British Empire's drug trade, which is an enormous part of this migration phenomenon.

Do you think people come here for any other reason than the fact that there is no survival as human beings in these countries? The reason is the collapse of potential relative population-density. And it is only explained, looking back at least 50 years, to understand what has gone on here. The only way to understand the drug epidemic is looking back at least 50 years to the British policies that have been unleashed.

LaRouche's New Bretton Woods Solution

Let us now shift to look at the answer. I planned to discuss the New Bretton Woods system with you today. Lyndon LaRouche, in the video clip you heard, explained that far better than I ever could, in great detail. That is the policy that has to be created.

When you start to think about what the necessary monetary system is, and how you engage in banking reform, and what policies to implement, you have to think of it backwards. You have to start from the standpoint of what you want the result to be. You don't start

Emigration from Mexico and Central America
(as of 2015)

Country	Population	In US (1st gen.)	%	In US (1st – 3rd gen.)	%
Mexico	125.9	11.5	9.1%	35.8	28.4%
Guatemala	16.3	0.9	5.5%	1.4	8.6%
Honduras	9.0	0.6	6.7%	0.9	10.0%
El Salvador	6.3	1.3	20.6%	2.2	34.9%

by discussing monetary policy. You start by saying: Okay, how are we going to increase potential relative population-density? You figure out what those policies are, and then you take a step.

Here's what I mean by working backward. Step four is, you increase the relative population-density, which requires advanced science like fusion, space sciences and so on. The way to achieve that is with step three, policies such as the Belt and Road Initiative, the great infrastructure projects, both regionally and globally, and so on. The way you can implement that is you require step two, a Hamiltonian system both internationally—such as the Asian Infrastructure Investment Bank or the BRICS New Development Bank—and nationally, you need a National Bank in every country to implement a Hamiltonian system.

To get to step two, you have to have a global Glass-Steagall; you have to have a global system of fixed exchange rates; you have to have exchange controls. Inside the United States, we have to return to FDR's Glass-Steagall. And you have to write off the vast majority of that $1.5 quadrillion cancer, as LaRouche was just explaining. And, of course, you do need step "0"— prosecute and jail those who are responsible for those policies. We wouldn't want to forget that.

The Americas

Let me just give you a quick bird's eye view of how such policies can and would work in one part of the world, which is in the Americas, and as part of the global World Land-Bridge perspective or the Belt and Road Initiative perspective, as we have been developing over decades now, in point of fact. The reason I

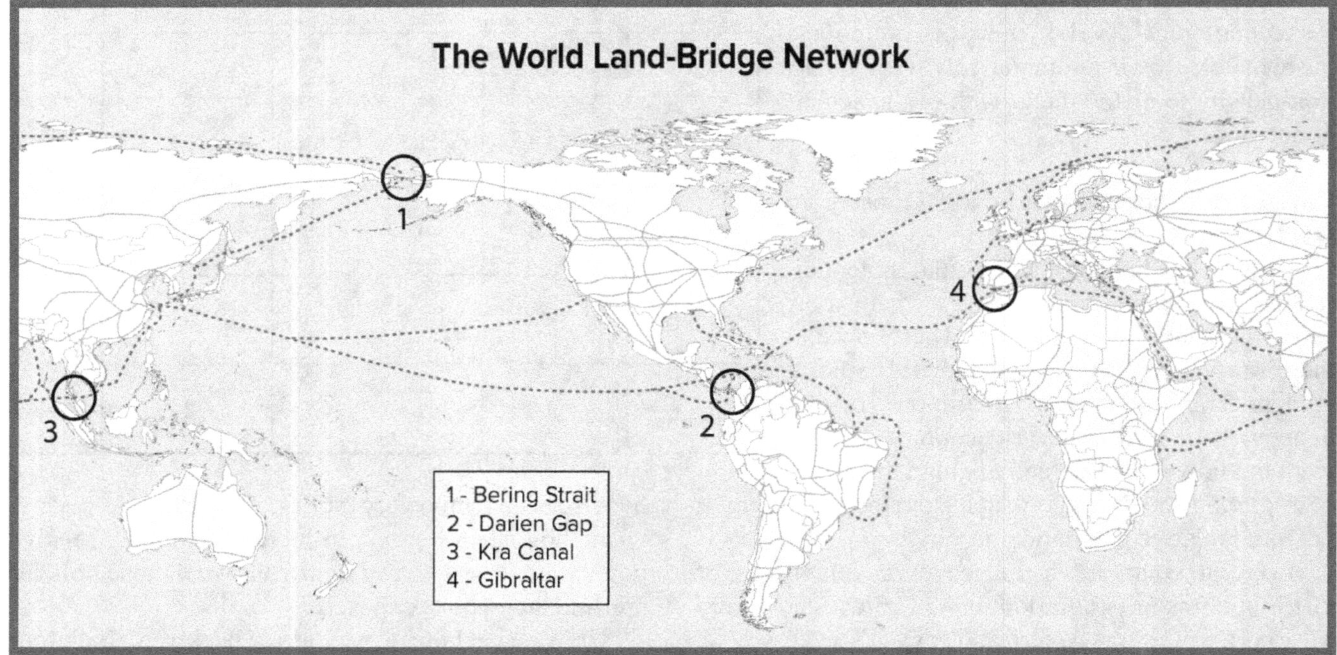

want to mention this, is that there are openings that have been created, a potential flank, by the election of Andrés Manuel López Obrador in Mexico, who has usefully extended an initiative to President Trump in the United States saying, "Hey, listen! You know what? Let's solve our problems of migration and drugs by development. Let's have joint development projects." Trump has responded quite favorably to that. López Obrador has also talked to the Chinese and said, "We're very interested in working with China on the Belt and Road."

The way this thing can work, and the only way it can work, is if you have a combination of the United States, Mexico, *and China*, working together on these projects. It's like a microcosm of what is required globally. But it's a very specific case where we can actually get—I'm convinced—the United States working with Mexico and China in this part of the world.

Now, I want to mention three specific projects out of many that we have discussed and presented, but these three in particular, because they speak to the issue of U.S.-Chinese cooperation as part of the global Four Powers.

One is, as you can see from this map [**Fig. 6**], the Global World Land-Bridge Network with not only the rail links, which link the Americas through the Darién Gap, labeled as Number 2, up through Mexico, the United States, Canada, Alaska, and through the Bering Strait Tunnel to Russia, labeled as Number 1. But, what you'll also see on this map is the extension, these blue dotted lines, of China's Maritime Silk Road proposal— the idea being that this must be extended across the Atlantic, into the Caribbean, through the expanded Panama Canal and the new, yet-to-be-built Nicaragua Grand Canal, and for trade across Asia.

Obviously, this network, this rail network in particular, requires the Chinese Belt and Road Initiative, but it also requires the active participation of the United States, not only for the U.S. portion, but for the investments in the work in other parts of the continent.

China has proposed new rail lines in Mexico, which the incoming Mexican government of López Obrador is studying carefully and hopefully will begin to develop. One is a rail route from a new port in Nayarit on the west coast of Mexico up through Ciudad Juárez (El Paso on the U.S. side), to connect to the U.S. rail grid. Another is a high-speed rail line from Mexico City to Querétaro; and a third, the most interesting one, is a trans-isthmian railroad—that's the Isthmus of Tehuantepec there—from the port of Coatzacoalcos on the Gulf Coast to Salina Cruz on the Pacific Coast, which would be a high-speed rail route with industrial corridors all along the way. That's one nested group of proposals which are international in scope.

This [**Fig. 7**], the Caribbean Basin Belt and Road proposals, which we have presented in our new World Land-Bridge report, involves on the one hand the Caribbean Maritime Silk Road routes, which go just west of Puerto Rico, the Mona Passage on the route to the Panama Canal. The idea here is that you really need to develop and build deep-water industrial ports in Ponce, Puerto Rico and Mariel, Cuba. Ponce, Puerto Rico is part of the United States. This would then serve—these two ports in particular—to link Gulf Coast and Atlantic Coast of the United States—the ports there—develop those ports which currently are most inadequate to the tasks of world trade; and of course through the entire Caribbean network, the Panama Canal, and through the Nicaraguan Canal.

So, that's another area of projects which directly involve Chinese-U.S. cooperation in this particular area of the world.

The Equator, The Shortcut to Outer Space

A third project, which I think is in one sense the most interesting, is the one indicated by these stars in Kourou, French Guiana and in Alcantara, Brazil. These are the two space launch sites which are the closest to the Equator of any launch sites anywhere on the planet—which is extremely advantageous, in terms of the physics of it, for space work and launch sites, to be right on the Equator.

These two launch sites should become the center of scientific development for the entire area, to emphatically include the training of the labor force in countries including in Central America, which are now being devastated by the drug trade and IMF policies; including in the Caribbean, which also requires that kind of upgrading; and also involving NASA and the United States and also the Chinese space mission. So, it's a perfect case of a science-driver policy, which will serve to benefit the entire region. And the Chinese have

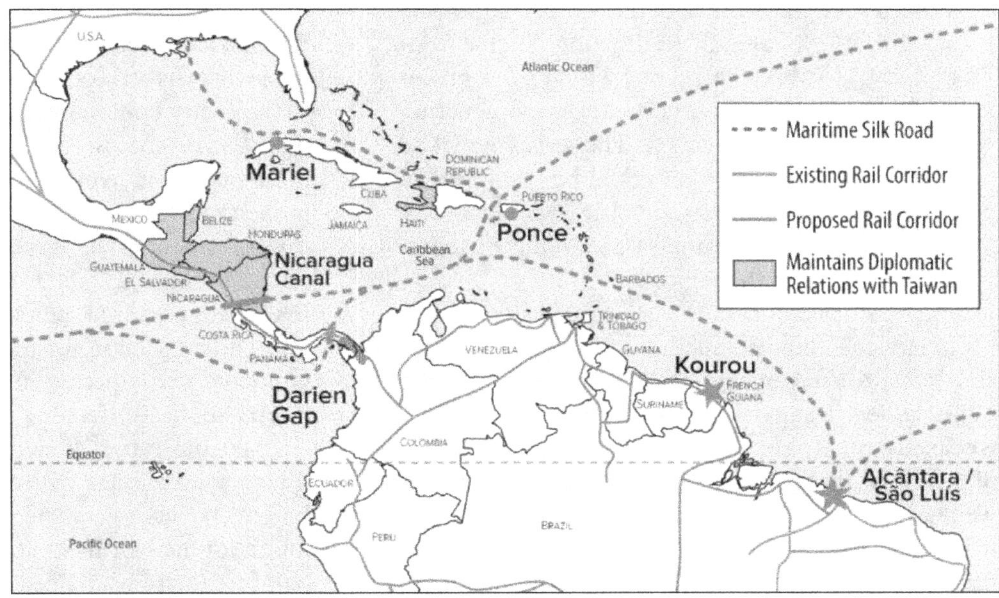

already stated explicitly—in their 2016 policy proposal for Ibero-America and the Caribbean—that they are in favor of this kind of scientific, space-scientific cooperation with the countries of Ibero-America in general.

So, this is something that is absolutely doable—with a change in the global policy. This only works if you have a New Bretton Woods. It only works as a way of forcing the creation of a New Bretton Woods and as a part of the Four Power agreements.

LaRouche, Reagan, López Portillo and Indira Gandhi

I want to conclude with a discussion of a specific case study of how history is made by ideas, of how LaRouche addressed the world crisis in the early 1980s, with his close collaboration simultaneously with the then President of Mexico López Portillo; with the then Prime Minister of India Indira Gandhi; and with the then President of the United States Ronald Reagan. And what LaRouche proposed, almost the moment Ronald Reagan was elected in November 1980. In December 1980, just a couple of weeks later, Lyndon LaRouche sent a confidential memorandum to Reagan and his team, proposing an approach to U.S.-Mexico relations, from the standpoint of the global changes that were required. What he said in that memo, among other things (this is just a brief quote from it) was:

Forging an "oil for technology" partnership with Mexico is only the first step in linking the advanced sector and the underdeveloped nations in a policy of global industrialization. Such a principled U.S.-Mexican accord would set a precedent which virtually every developing nation will want to replicate.... The crisis-wracked Central American region could be stabilized in the only way possible—by U.S.-Mexican collaboration to set in motion economic development projects in the region.

LaRouche then pursued this idea. López Portillo and Ronald Reagan met just weeks later, on Jan. 5, 1981, when Reagan was still President-elect. Two weeks after that, López Portillo travelled to India. One of the topics that had been discussed with Reagan—and we learned about it in private discussions afterwards, as it wasn't announced—was that López Portillo would make an effort to bring India on board this policy-approach, with which Reagan concurred, the outlines of which had been established by LaRouche.

López Portillo did in fact travel to India on Jan. 19 of that year and the LaRouche movement prepared a special report called, "The India Which José López Portillo Will Find." We published that report in both English and Spanish prior to López Portillo's arrival; we got it out everywhere, and that report did in fact help shape that meeting, which was decisive for the development of the strategic situation.

Further discussion among these triangular forces, which LaRouche had set in motion with ideas, was briefly suspended or delayed by two developments. First, the attempted assassination of Ronald Reagan by Hinckley on March 30, 1981 (hardly in office). And a month later on April 27, 1981, an attempted assassination of Indira Gandhi. But nonetheless, in June 8-9, 1981, López Portillo and Reagan did meet; Reagan was sufficiently recovered for that.

López Portillo invited Reagan to the first-ever and the only time a North-South meeting was held. He called it in Cancún, Mexico. It was a North-South dialogue. Reagan accepted to go there in June 1981. And within six weeks, Lyndon LaRouche had issued a detailed memorandum for what every head of state attending that meeting needed to know. We published that under the title of "The Principles of Statecraft for Defining a New North-South Order." After this, there were the meetings in 1982 of LaRouche with López Portillo, meetings with Indira Gandhi, and of course, LaRouche's famous *Operation Juárez* document.

The Principles of Statecraft

I want to focus on what LaRouche said in this paper, to make my concluding point, really the central point, which we saw in the LaRouche exposition just a moment ago as well, on LaRouche's method: His approach to how to deal with these problems. Because in this document, "The Principles of Statecraft," 76 pages, the first sentence is the following. He says, "This report has been prepared chiefly to provide needed background knowledge for members and advisors of governments participating in the scheduled October 1981 North-South Conference in Cancún, Mexico."

And the report concludes, at the very end of the report, it concludes with an actual draft memorandum. LaRouche has a very specific proposal. It's a draft resolution for the North-South Conference in Mexico, eight points, exactly what needs to be done. The participants, by the way, ended up being 20 or so heads of state: López Portillo, Ronald Reagan, Indira Gandhi, Ferdinand Marcos of the Philippines, Zhao Ziyang of China, Forbes Burnham of Guyana, Chadli Bendjedid of Algeria; and then, very unfortunately, Margaret Thatcher of the United Kingdom; equally or more unfortunately, François Mitterrand of France, and so forth; those were the people who were there.

LaRouche begins by saying this a message of the knowledge you need to have, to do what you need to do. He concludes with a tactical proposal. I can remember him saying on many occasions—probably many of you do as well—when asked for the tactics to deal with a situation, "Tactics, you want tactics? I can give you a million tactics. I can give you tactics every two minutes, if you want. That's not the problem. The problem is how do you think? How do you develop the required tactical approach that actually functions to change from one global geometry to another?"

LaRouche, in the intervening pages, the 70 pages in between the beginning and the end of this report, addresses those issues. I want to make two or three points: First, he discusses the issue of potential relative population-density, and he says the following:

The relative power of a culture to provide the development of its individual members is delimited by what we shall explain as its potential relative population-density.... If the population exceeds the potential relative population-density of such a fixed culture, there must be periodic genocidal catastrophes resulting from refusal to change the culture from a "traditional" mode.

And then he goes on to say,

Most specific cultures have resisted the required changes.... most of the specific cultures which have resisted cultural progress, have resisted advances in technology, have either been assimilated by conquest, or have become extinct, or have degenerated into lower forms of barbarism and even savagery.

This conception, just outlined, subsumes both the special achievements and threatened imminent collapse of European civilization.

So, if that phrase about "descent into lower forms of barbarism and even savagery" sounds like what's happening today, you're absolutely correct. LaRouche put his finger right on the issue even back then—where it all was heading if the situation was not changed.

He then turns to what he calls a special concept of morality that is required to understand economic science. He says,

Let us now embark upon what may be to some the most exciting mental excursion of exploration they have experienced to date. Let us show not only from whence economic science actually originates, a far different origin than they might have presumed, but show also that a scientific knowledge is efficiently and usefully subsumed by the authority of an economic science defined in this way.

How the Universe Reacts to Human Action

He then goes on to discuss where the concept of morality, which is coincident with a concept of immortality, where it derives from: "Each act by the individual is an act upon a lawfully ordered universe. That universe, by virtue of its lawful composition, reacts to the action upon it, generating ripples of consequence throughout the width and duration of present and time to come." He continues:

Each act is characterized, therefore, by an associated generative principle, a principle which, as a notion, defines the ordered succession of chain-reaction ripples extended outward from the action itself. Each act by an individual is in that way akin to the act of a legislature, in that it "legislates" a definite chain of consequences. The character of that chain of consequences, in respect to the cumulative effects in width and duration of present and time to come, is the true character of the individual action.

Having so defined the nature of causality in the physical universe, and therefore in the economic universe, which after all is part of the physical universe, or it is nothing—having traced the origin of real causality to the issue of morality and ideas, and the actions which individuals take consequent to those ideas and that sense of morality, he concludes his argument with a really stunning discussion of what economic science actually is. LaRouche continues,

This economic science is focused most immediately upon the interdependence of advances in technology and maintaining and increasing the potential relative population-density which a society may achieve through the efforts of its own members.... *The subject of economic science is the increased power of Reason in the individual member of society.*

And that, I believe, is the absolutely crucial concept which is required of us as organizers to be induced for the mental reproduction, the conceptual reproduction of those that we are organizing, for people to be able to not only understand what must be done; why we must stop the coup against Trump; why we must have a New Bretton Woods; why there has to be a Four-Powers Agreement. Not only to understand why those are scientific requirements. But from that concept as well—which comes exclusively from LaRouche's work in the modern era—to derive the requisite sense of identity and morality to purposefully guide us to achieve those results. We have the opportunity to do this at this moment; we simply have to think like LaRouche, as he demonstrated to us in the video excerpt which we just saw. Thank you.

JUNE 12, 2008

Free Trade Vs. National Interest: The Economics Debate about Russia

by Lyndon H. LaRouche, Jr.

The pattern of cooperation among Russia, China, and India, is presently the pivot of any potential resistance to the present, London-led drive toward establishing the global fascism of a utopian, frankly imperial "New Tower of Babel." This is a drive which is currently expressed as the former British Prime Minister Tony Blair's proposed, imperialist, ideological, post-, anti-Westphalian hegemony in western and central continental Europe. This still continuing, London-centered attempt to transform all of continental and central Europe into virtually a captive British colony, through such schemes as the proposed Lisbon Treaty, is complemented by the force of an implicitly treasonous hegemony of the mole-like, London-centered, financier influences behind current policy-shaping influences of leading elements of current U.S. national policy-shaping. This reflects a degree of British leading press and British control over the combined regular and irregular financing of U.S. Presidential election-campaigns, which is so large today that it would stun the many voters who actually confronted themselves with the evidence showing how much they have been manipulated in their voting by such foreign power, thus far.

In Russia, and among its principal Asian partners, the included reactions to this are to be recognized in a currently evolving, asymmetric strategy of self-defense against current British imperialism—and those nations' governments do know that this is British imperi-

alism. That current British imperial role will bring crucial reactions by Russia and its partners. These reactions prompt my increasing concern about the part which liberal elements still occupy in Russia's own economic policy. My concern for all three—Russia, China, and India—among those nations, and also others, centers on currently menacing ambiguities posed by that influence of free-trade ideology inside Russia itself, which is, itself, an added threat to Russia's own national interest—and therefore, also ours—still today, a threat which persists despite the intended victims' concern to check such influence by alien interests.

The matter which I put before this audience now, takes our attention to the heart of the urgently needed remedies for the gravest strategic crisis in all of modern world history: the presently onrushing, greatest economic crisis since Europe's Fourteenth Century. This is that present, global, hyper-inflationary crisis which has now entered its succession of terminal phases.

This crisis itself could be overcome, but it could not be solved by any effort which was limited to merely reforming the present world monetary-financial system. In the very important matter which I present for discussion before this international audience in these pages, we shall consider the uniquely required remedy for the cause of this crisis.

This requires that we recognize the factor of widespread, crucial, strategic and historical illiteracy respecting real (i.e., physical) economy, even among high-ranking, ostensibly well-informed circles. This has been a kind of illiteracy which has been popularized

Editor's note: First published in the July 4, 2008 issue of *Executive Intelligence Review*.

EIRNS/Rachel Douglas

If a horror similar to, or worse than Europe's 14th-Century New Dark Age is to be averted, LaRouche advises, a four-power agreement among the governments of the U.S.A., Russia, China, and India, must be achieved, to reform the world's economic and monetary systems, and to reach into the coming half-century. Here, LaRouche, in Moscow, with his friend, Prof. Stanislav Menshikov, May 2007.

as that reigning popular belief which has been planted among the relevant portion of that trans-Atlantic white-collar generation, the generation which was born during the 1945-1958 interval. This illiteracy is expressed in the form of a belief planted deep within them, as also younger generations, a belief expressed as a militant form of ignorance, ignorance of the axiomatic-like presumptions which lurk today, often unsuspected, as relics of influences deeply embedded in the psyches of the living, influences expressing the residues, transmitted within successive generations, of problematic experiences dating from centuries or more in the recent history of present cultures, even, sometimes, carried over from truly ancient times.

This situation confronts us with two categorical challenges. First, there is the fact that a powerful political force, the presently reigning international financial oligarchy, is so much opposed to the only existing choice of any actual remedy for this crisis, that those specific kinds of oligarchical interests would appear to prefer to see this planet (including their own nation) in Hell, rather than accept the only available option for remedying the currently onrushing, general, financial-monetary breakdown of the economy of the world as a whole. Second, there is also the complication contrib-

uted by the widespread honest ignorance of those principles of economy which must be considered for adoption, if the world is to escape the presently onrushing horrors of the present situation, horrors which reach far, far beyond the matter of those soaring gasoline and Winter heating-fuel prices to be expected, if the present policies of our own and other leading governments are allowed to continue as they are.

To save humanity from the presently onrushing threat of an early general breakdown-crisis which would ricochet throughout the planet, we must abandon currently popular opinions about certain relevant, current events. We must abandon both "information theory" and that recently acquired habit of mere "googling" which has become widely employed today as a proposed substitute for actually thinking. We must view all of now globally extended European civilization, with its intervals of increasingly convulsive, global internal developments, as gripped by a single, dynamical process; we must view this world-wide process as a process among respectively sovereign nations with sovereign cultures; and, we must view that process among nations in the following, dynamical manner.

What must occur soon, if a horror which would be worse than Europe's Fourteenth-Century so-called "New Dark Age" is to be averted, must be the formation of an initial organizing committee composed of the governments of the U.S.A., Russia, China, and India,[1] a committee whose agreement to what needs to be adopted as certain common principles of reform, principles which will serve as the needed catalyst for a general, more or less global agreement to a reform committed to certain principles of global cooperation among a majority of the world's nation-states. This reform must be essentially global, and must be crafted to serve as a process of reform to be continued during a coming half-century interval.[2]

My recommendation is, that the U.S.A. must become prepared, soon, to volunteer its participation in

---

1. And, also, for strategic reasons, early during the continuing process, Japan, Korea, and Mongolia.

2. A cycle of fifty years may be a long wait for some, if not for an old man of eighty-five. For the purposes of addressing a world crisis of the present type, the man of eighty-five has the right outlook.

this four-power initiative. This recommendation will astonish some; but, none the less, it is indispensable if civilization is to be preserved. At the present moment, what I propose does indeed appear to be an unlikely development for the near future. However, my advantage in this matter, is that I have clearly in view, as most other leading figures and circles do not, the kind of blows which the presently onrushing, global economic-breakdown-crisis is about to deliver to the U.S. economy and its political process. Current history affords the U.S.A. no real option for survival, but that which I propose here, if it wishes to survive the presently onrushing phase of the ongoing crisis.

In this report, I emphasize the specific kind of practical, problematic implications which the process of considering such an effort presents to the government of Russia, for example. However, what I write here also has a more general relevance for all parties, including many in addition to the four which I have proposed to serve as an initiating committee for this global economic-recovery effort.

Restate the general argument for this action by the four indicated leading nations, as follows.

We must examine this presently ongoing span of unfolding modern world history, as a single, unified process of coherent development among what should be regarded, nonetheless, paradoxically, as being properly viewed as, respectively, essentially sovereign nations.

For example: We must discover the efficient coherence which is curiously hidden by what the current great majority of educated and barely educated opinion, alike, regards as separate factors of development, and even separate concerns and developments. In contemplating the proposed rescue mission for this planet, we must regard history as being like a complex, higher form of a living organization, whose organs interact with the built-in intent of an organic-like, common effect, an effect expressed as the unitary function of that organism as a whole. This is a function which is not homeostatic, but *dynamic* in Gottfried Leibniz's and Bernhard Riemann's sense of the term *dynamic*. Thus, we see modern history itself as a coherently lawful process of successive, alternating movements of rise and decline of civilization, as a process subsuming the process of relations among the world's present, seemingly contradictory set of respectively sovereign cultures as a whole.

To begin that investigation, consider the particular form of currently ongoing, "geopolitical" challenge

this presents to Russia's policy-shaping.

Look now at the case of Russia. Take into account some essential features inherited from the experience of the Soviet Union.

The Present Irony of Soviet Communism

Ironically, the emergence of Soviet Russia as a state power under the leadership of V.I. Lenin, confronted that new government with the desire, then, to rebuild an avowedly Communist Russia's agro-industrial economy, by building it around the successful model of practice of what Russia had viewed then as "American capitalist methods." Praise of "American methods" from sources at that time, was emphasized, on various occasions, as during the first five years of that government, by such leaders of that moment as both of the restively cooperating rivals V.I. Lenin and L.D. Trotsky.[3] These were "the American methods" which Russia had witnessed in the great agro-industrial power shown by the World War I period of mobilization of the United States' economy, a reflection of what was also to be seen, since about 1876, by notable Russian leaders in the way in which Germany's agro-industrial power had leaped ahead through the adoption, at about the same time, of what had been a kernel of American-System-like reforms led by Chancellor Otto von Bismarck.

Throughout the entire sweep of Soviet history, from 1917 to 1989, all the critical issues of national-economic policy for that nation's patriots, were centered, in fact, on a debate of the issue of the systemic differences between the American nationalist and the British-Liberal-imperial models of the economy. What were the methods to which the young Soviet Union's otherwise avowed followers of Karl Marx might, then turn? Winston Churchill, like the avowed Luciferian Aleister Crowley, like the avowed fascist H.G. Wells, and the avowed radically Malthusian genocidalist and avowed nuclear and biological-warfare mass-murderer Bertrand Russell, in their time together, had shared motives, and tastes more or less peculiar to their own such circles; but, these sorts of ethics were scarcely what might be properly identified

---

3. The Soviet economist Preobrazhensky's notion of "primitive socialist accumulation," introduced during the early through later 1920s, was a product of the same provocative, historical irony. This time, Preobrazhensky reflected the economist Rosa Luxemburg's more insightful treatment of the concept of imperialism as a matter of a system of international loans, as the American scholar Herbert Feis was to support the same conclusion of Rosa Luxemburg with his own studies later.

by decent people as moral scruples.[4]

It should have been obvious to modern historians, that, in general, Russian leading political and strategic thought, generally, has not yet resolved, even at this late date, what confronts it as the paradox of a Russia viewing the actuality of the relevant, presently continuing, historical conflict of its outlook on the English-speaking world, that between the U.S.A. constitutional tradition, as typified by President Franklin Roosevelt, and the British empire's system, still today. This confusion, often found among Russian circles of the past, is reenforced by the fact that the so-called "Wall Street" faction in the U.S.A. is the principal expression of the British imperial tradition of such as Aaron Burr, which is still operating prominently, today, from within the leading institutions of the U.S.A.

The legacy of Karl Marx's role as an intellectually confused pawn of Britain's Lord Palmerston, can be found even today in the confusion among both Marxists and non-Marxists alike, on the matter of the conflict between British and American political economy and history.

The included source of that specific kind of confusion, which is to be seen not only in Russia, but in European thought generally, has been, most notably, the long-standing failure by the socialist movements generally, as also by other observers, to recognize the relevant truth about Karl Marx's role as, implicitly, an intellectually confused pawn of the British Foreign Office of Jeremy Bentham's protégé; a Marx who, in his own time in London, was under the management of Bentham's heir and immediate successor, Lord Palmerston.[5]

The principal source of this confusion, has been the socialists', and others' stubborn refusal, whether as either avowed Marxists, or his customary, present-day and former opponents from leading political circles, to acknowledge Karl Marx's role as in a fully documented position as an agent-in-fact of Palmerston's own Young Europe organization of Palmerston agents Mazzini et al. This aspect of Marx's own (and relevant others') credulities has been largely responsible for the pathetic confusion, whether or not Marx himself was fully conscious of that arrangement. Such has been the state of confusion among both Marxists and anti-Marxists alike on this matter of the actual, persisting conflict between British and American political-economy and history. This has been the root of much Russian confusion (and that of many others, too) on this point, even at high-ranking levels, even in the present day.

Since "the Fall of the Wall," in 1989, which occurred during the term of U.S. President George H.W. Bush,[6] the insane, implicitly hyper-inflationary policies and practices which had already been imposed, as a trend, under U.S. Federal Reserve Chairman Alan Greenspan, have continued to prevail up to the present

---

4. We must never be so silly as to suggest that Britain's Churchill and Bertrand Russell acted with moral "sincerity" in their argument for launching a "preventive nuclear attack" on the Soviet Union, as Russell presented his proposal publicly in September 1946. Russell's actual intent, as he confessed publicly later, was: "As for public life, when I first became politically conscious Gladstone and Disraeli still confronted each other amid Victorian solidities, the British Empire seemed eternal, a threat to British naval supremacy was unthinkable, the country was aristocratic, rich, and growing richer.... For an old man, with such a background, it is difficult to feel at home in a world of ... American supremacy." Bertrand Russell, *The Impact of Science on Society*, 1953. Russell's intention, like Churchill's, was to outflank, and ultimately destroy the work of that U.S. Franklin Roosevelt Presidency seen by both as a threat to the British empire.

5. Marx once wrote a treatise in which he claimed to have exposed the man who was actually his master of that period of time, Lord Palmerston, as "a Russian spy." One might wonder, who, actually, put Marx up to that job!

6. In February 1983, I had warned of a threatened economic collapse of the Soviet Union, as likely to occur "within about five years," should President Reagan propose, and the Soviet government reject cooperation of the type which I expected that President Reagan would proffer. Later in the Spring of that year, after the President had proffered the SDI and discussion of this had been summarily rejected, I repeated that forecast publicly. That remained a standing forecast, as repeatedly stated publicly by me, through my October 12, 1988 Berlin TV warning of an imminent chain-reaction collapse of the Comecon system, beginning in Poland, during early 1989. I had developed, and publicly circulated my first long-range forecast of this type in 1960-61, warning, that unless corrective measures were taken to deal with the trend established at the close of the 1950s, we must expect a series of monetary crises during the second half of the 1960s, with the threat of a breakdown of the then present monetary system about the end of the 1960s, or beginning of the 1970s, I have made several such forecasts, and have never erred in any among them. This success has been a matter of a method contrary to those intrinsically incompetent "race-track handicapping"-like methods used by the usual professional statistical forecasters. "Yes, or no?" forecasts of events by a specific date, are always products of intrinsically incompetent methods employed.

moment of writing, even under Greenspan's pathetically confused successor, Ben Bernanke. Similarly, the Presidency of Russia's President Yeltsin continued to be under the influence of this London-steered, ruinous, Anglo-American line of Greenspan and his successors, through, and beyond the time of the LTCM/Russian Bond scandal of August-September 1998.

However, since then, even with those very significant, later improvements in direction of Russia's economic policy, under the Presidency of Vladimir Putin, the essential features of the conflict between Russia's vital national physical-economic interests and the ruinous influence of predatory British monetarism, has not been fully resolved, conceptually, in Russia, to the present day—or, by most among those from western and central Europe who prefer Britain's part to the constitutional tradition of the U.S.A., dupes who, when they are in leading positions, are usually pawns of British intelligence services.

After all, intelligent, well-informed U.S. nationals know that Britain's royally beknighted former U.S. President George H.W. Bush is, like his father, that late Prescott Bush, who joined Britain's Montagu Norman in backing Adolf Hitler's cause, among those sympathizers of British imperialism, who, often, might as well be, then as now, tantamount to British agents in the practical implications of much of the practice of such sympathizers at sundry later times.

However, in the meantime, after the events of 1989, my insight into a needed new direction of Russian thinking in these matters, had been, already introduced by my wife and others among my own, and my associates' published work. These forecasts and related proposals were already introduced in part by relevant circles during the early through middle 1990s, post-Gorbachev, Yeltsin Russia. My own view was introduced by such notably influential intellectual figures as the brilliantly creative physicist Pobisk Kuznetsov, who was among the first prominent figures, then and there, to grasp certain leading implications of my teaching of the principles of physical economy, as opposed to any of the sundry, popularized forms of monetarism.

For example, by 1996, as illustrated by a meeting in which I participated as a member of the panel, in Moscow, there was a professionally and politically prestigious body of Russia's economists which met with me there and in other locations, prepared to approach the U.S.A. for the kind of reforms which would have been feasible at that time. The support for such reform collapsed, largely as a result of the corrupt influence of then-Vice-President Al Gore within the context of the U.S. re-election campaign of President Clinton, all of which coincided with the course of Gore-backed Yeltsin's campaign for his own re-election as President.

However, even with the beneficial shift under the Presidency of Vladimir Putin, the lingering influence of British, radically free-trade variety of monetarist dogmas, although diminished as a visible factor in Russia's policy-shaping, has persisted as an opposing, crippling factor of influence, despite now former President Putin's effort to establish the policies needed for a sustainable attempt at rebuilding not only Russia's economy, but to accept the goal, in practice, of creating the urgently needed, new, Bretton Woods-like reform of the world credit-system.

Admittedly, under the conditions in the U.S. government at the moment this report is written, the hope for such a reform of U.S. practice might appear to be far-fetched. I am not so pessimistic as to share that view. Shocking developments are already under way; these are times when many kinds of seemingly impossible changes will become probable.

Such is real history and its national and international complexities of policy-shaping up to the present time. Russia's freeing itself from the perilous ambiguities of efforts to balance Russia's national physical-economic interests against the residual, but still dangerous influence of Russia's own menacing monetarists, is a problem which must be addressed, if Russia's government is to be enabled to play its own crucial, unique role as a crucially needed partner among the four powers, the U.S.A., Russia, China, and India: the set of powers which must provide the core around which the majority of the human race rallies to rescue our immediately imperilled planet as a whole today.

I limit my discussion in this present publication, to reflect the conditions of what I can see and know with the authority of virtual certainty, as the principled nature of the problematic features in the publicly stated domestic policies of Russia accordingly.

I emphasize the importance of my taking up this specific issue now, under what are, presently, the actual circumstances of an accelerating global general breakdown-crisis of the present international monetary-financial system. The relevance of this can be demonstrated to best effect, by limiting the proposals presented here to the matter of considering the special role which potential cooperation between the U.S.A. on the one side, and Russia, China, and India, on the other, must play, if an actual recovery of our planet could emerge out of the presently onrushing, global breakdown-crisis of the present world monetary system.

That action is urgent, as I emphasize in the following chapters of this report.

I. A Unique Chance for Recovery

The present world monetary-financial system in its present form, is in an absolutely hopeless, terminal condition. Contrary to popular mythologies, without a new system, the present world situation will be a hopeless one for all concerned. Since developments of the early 1970s, from August 15, 1971 on, the present global, monetarist system has no longer been controlled by the U.S.A., but, increasingly, since the mid-1970s, by a petro-dollar-centered, Anglo-Dutch Liberal, floating-exchange-rate, financier-oligarchical system, a neo-Venetian-style system, whose control is presently, nominally centered, politically and financially, in London, Amsterdam, and Rotterdam.

As the case of British control of much of the current financing, and policy shaping of the pre-U.S. Presidential campaigns of the Democratic and Republican parties, illustrates the point, we must accept the fact, that all major policy-shaping by the U.S. government and major press policy today, is being currently shaped so far, predominantly, through the pivot and spigot of the petroleum "spot market" and its overlap with British intelligence's currently infamous military-intelligence operations' arm, known as BAE.

Take the particular case of London's top-down control of the U.S. Democratic Party's current Presidential campaign through such channels as the otherwise marginal figure of current Democratic Party Chairman Howard Dean's putative owner, London's George Soros. This case attests to the effects today of a subversive process of U.S. decline to London's intended imperial advantage, an advantage which may be traced largely to the August 1971 breakup of the Bretton Woods system, and the subsequent launching of the 1970s oil-price hoax.[7]

This British subversion was continued through the systemic destruction of the U.S. physical economy by the 1977-1981 program of the destruction of the U.S. physical economy through the David Rockefeller-backed Trilateral Commission; and, continued, more recently, through the chain-reaction ruin of the economies of continental Europe through the chain-reaction effects of the Thatcher government's thrusting the Maastricht Treaty down the throat of Germany and other nations of continental Europe. This bent is typified by the Rockefeller Foundation's proposal, for Benito Mussolini-style fascism for the U.S.A. today, in the Foundation's scheme featuring such figures New York Mayor Michael Bloomberg and California Governor Arnold Schwarzenegger. This is also a scheme echoing those practices of the medieval Fourteenth-Century "New Dark Age" which halved the number of existing parishes in Europe, and reduced the population of Europe, rapidly, by about one-third.

Now, the design of the contested Lisbon Treaty, although rejected by a popular majority's vote in Ireland, still threatens us all with both the threat of the early, fascist-like extinction of virtually all sovereign government by any nation of western and central continental Europe, and by the use of a London-controlled residue of that Treaty, as a military force aimed for the subjugation of all Asia and Russia, too. This brings the world to the verge of the reign of an Anglo-Dutch Liberal financier-oligarchical tyranny over the world, a tyranny which, if established, would be an echo, indeed, of Europe's Fourteenth-Century plunge into a new dark age. Such a descent into a dark age which would be accompanied by a spread and escalation of the pattern of warfare, including emphasis on "shock and awe" raining from the stratosphere, a scheme into which Britain's Tony Blair et al. levered the U.S. under President George W. "Patsy" Bush, that on the pretext of "9-11."

This new quality of present threat to all civilization arises now, when the outstanding financial claims of what is, presently, a London-directed world imperial system, have reached a point of decadence beyond all

---

7. The control of the Democratic Party's National Committee, and of the Presidential nomination campaign of Senator Barack Obama by funds channeled largely by London's George Soros, is typical of London's large degree of control over all such campaigns, and of a large part of the U.S. financial system otherwise. This change actually began with the assassination of President John F. Kennedy, and the Autumn 1967 British Sterling crisis followed by its echoes in the changes introduced under U.S. President Lyndon Johnson, on March 1, 1968.

EIRNS/Brian McAndrews

Despite the unequivocal "No!" by the Irish people to the fascist-like Lisbon Treaty, Europe is still threatened by the attempt to impose a London-directed supranational dictatorship, as the world plunges into economic and social chaos. Here, LaRouche PAC organizers celebrate the Irish victory, in Philadelphia, Pa., June 2008.

calculation, that by its intrinsic nature, that far beyond any amounts of explicit financial claims involved.

This present monetary-financial system is so structured, that its menacing state of presently accelerating hyper-inflation, with its increasing rates and amounts of financial collapse, could be terminated in only one of two probable outcomes: either by, 1.), a complete, hyper-inflationary breakdown of the present system, or, 2.), by the intervention of a powerful combination among governments, to put the system into receivership for a fundamental redesign as echoing a Bretton Woods system of the type which President Franklin Roosevelt (but not that of Britain's John Maynard Keynes) had actually intended at the Bretton Woods conference of 1944.

The consequences of a general breakdown are such that no truly sane and intelligent government could refuse to consider the action which I am proposing. However, not all those governments are truly sane, or even intelligent, in respect to these economic matters, and few presently incumbent governments are truly competent in today's real state of world affairs, respecting what are now, most immediately, crucially essential matters of economic policies of practice.

Parenthetically, imagine for a moment, that the world would not continue its present plunge into an early breakdown of its financial systems, a collapse which would now occur, were there no reorganization of the world's credit system of the kind which I prescribe: what is currently proposed would echo, if in a manner reflecting the change in capabilities of modern weaponry, the Fourteenth-Century imperial tyranny of a Venetian financier oligarchy. Such an echo of that Fourteenth-Century horror, would be launched through newly reigning mechanisms, of city-based banking like that proposed by the U.S. Rockefeller Foundation behind the Mussolini-style schemes of New York's Mayor Bloomberg, a scheme echoing the monstrous, medieval folly of the Venice-created, Fourteenth-Century, Lombard banking-system.

That will not occur. The crash is in process. Only a general outbreak of what would become planet-wide, even nuclear warfare, would produce a different "scenario" than our intention is focussed upon in the mainstream of this present report.

The urgently needed re-design of the world's monetary system, includes the requirement of what would turn out to have been, simply, cancelling what is presently the greatest, intrinsically speculative, unproductive portion of the present, nominally outstanding, financial debt (as typified by the case of so-called "hedge funds," or, in Germany, "locusts"), and replacing the present world monetary system with a new one, one modeled upon President Franklin Roosevelt's 1944 design for the Bretton Woods system (not the crucially flawed, Keynesian substitute for Roosevelt's system). Such a new system requires concerted, cooperative action by nations which, in efforts combined for common action, represent the most vital interests of not only a majority of the human population today, but the future of virtually all of humanity for generations yet to come.[8]

---

8. What President Franklin Roosevelt had intended, during the 1944 Bretton Woods conference, was to have been a nested set of treaty agreements with the U.S. constitutional credit-system. What was

As indicated at the outset of this report, such a timely, needed reform would be impossible without the initiative of cooperation among four, selected, keystone nations: the U.S.A., Russia, China, and India. An appropriate initiative by those four, would assuredly draw many other nations into membership in the same cooperating body for the needed, concerted, immediate action, and for agreements on long-term reform of the international credit-system. Such cooperation would represent sufficient, forceful political and related power, to bring about the presently, urgently needed reforms for economic recovery of the world system.

For the purpose of bringing about that urgently needed reform, we must recognize that the U.S.A. represents an economy of European culture, Russia one of Eurasian cultural history, and China and India, chiefly Asian cultures of, respectively, significantly different cultural characteristics. A similar challenge is presented by the sovereign characteristics of other prospective partners. This must be a system of agreements among nation-states, echoing the 1648 Peace of Westphalia, not the imperialist scheme of Anglo-Dutch-Liberal-dominated "free trade" and "globalization," which latter has been intended by such plotters as the government of either Prime Minister Margaret Thatcher's authorship of the Maastricht atrocity, or those of Prime Minister Tony Blair's government.

Contrary to such silly utopians as the current dupes of "globalist" and related "Malthusian" propaganda, these cultures must not be put under the law of a single supranational government. The nations can be, and must be united in purpose and common endeavor among sovereigns, but it must be among sovereigns. That must be done through adoption of certain common aims of mankind; but, the perfect sovereignty of the sovereign nation-state in its law and cultural characteristics, is the most essential among those common aims. Without that factor of sovereignty, the remainder of the effort would ultimately fail to reach any acceptable quality of common economic goals.

No new Tower of Babel wanted, *please! Nor a new,*

changed, by President Truman's agreement with the Winston Churchill he admired so much, was an agreement among monetary systems of a type adapted to a Keynes proposal which President Roosevelt had rejected at Bretton Woods. The special importance of the U.S.A.'s reaching an agreement with Russia, China, and India, as keystone partners now, is to create a "New Bretton Woods" agreement on the Franklin Roosevelt, 1944, not the Truman model.

presumably Fabian league of Cities of the Plain.

Efficient institutions of defense remain needed, as a precaution, but, contrary to Prime Minister Blair's government's role in the launching of the presently continuing warfare in Southwest Asia (and other places), not preemption, and never the infantile folly of high-flying "shock and awe." Proper defense in the true sense of the terms, including strategic defense, remains necessary for as far forward as we might foresee in practical terms today. But, with the quality of weaponry, and its warfare already existing, and advancing still today, we must emphasize again that the practice of preventive warfare, or, of conducting, or planning long wars like that which a lying Prime Minister Tony Blair promoted in Southwest Asia, contrary the warnings of Dr. David Kelley, is criminal, and should be treated as such.

Under such an urgently needed reform, the military policy of today's world must be a predicate of the principle of the 1648 Peace of Westphalia. Those of contrary persuasion occupying positions of great power, are to be considered criminals by virtue of the inherent effect of their intention. The worst such are those who associate such military policies with the imitation of a "Tower of Babble" called "Globalization," or the reduction of the human population by half or more, as such genocide vastly beyond the ambitions of Hitler, as proposed, still now, by Britain's Prince Philip and his batty World Wildlife Fund, and are to be treated as lunatics, or criminals.

The American System Itself

The specific and indispensable role of the U.S.A.'s acceptance of such a reform as that which I affirm here, is not merely a matter of choosing the precedent set by President Franklin Roosevelt. The crucial fact of the matter is, the fact that the United Kingdom, and most of the principal nations of western and central continental Europe, are either parliamentary, or quasi-parliamentary systems based upon, and inherently subject to Liberal monetary systems. It is, as I have indicated above, the specific, distinctive, constitutional characteristic of the U.S. constitutional ("Hamiltonian") definition of a sovereign currency-credit system, rather than a Western European-style monetary system, which is crucial for the success of the now urgently needed, prosperous, physical-economic recovery of the planet as a whole.

Therefore, in short, the objective must be to have the four proposed initiators (the U.S.A., Russia, China, and India) form the core of the larger set of nations which undertakes the initiating obligations for a treaty-agreement pivoted on the conception of a credit-system, instead of a monetary system. This shall be a treaty agreement, echoing the principle of the 1648 Peace of Westphalia, among a set of nations of differing internal cultural and other characteristics. This will serve, thus, as the initiating of the new, multi-cultural international credit-system, during the time the world's present monetary-financial system is being reorganized in bankruptcy.

The fact that the U.S. Constitutional system was created as a credit-system, rather than a monetary system, is a matter of crucial importance for any nation which wishes a feasible solution to the catastrophe now already descending upon it. The needed new system of world credit, required to stabilize prices, could be readily established, according to U.S. Constitutional law, by the device of a U.S. return to its Constitutional principle respecting the nature of its uttered currency and credit.

The *Constitutional U.S. system* is a credit-system, not a monetary system. Credit, and the uttering of currency based upon the lawful credit of nation-states, is the only possible, systematic form of escape from the current effects of the 1970s superceding of the Franklin Roosevelt-designed U.S. fixed-exchange-rate system, and going to that Anglo-Dutch Liberal floating-exchange-rate system which has brought about the world's presently onrushing storm of a general, intrinsically hyper-inflationary break-down crisis.

There are two relevant, exemplary ways in which Constitutional money and related Federal credit can be generated by the U.S.A. The first, by consent of Congress (e.g., the House of Representatives) to authorize the U.S. Presidency (e.g., the Secretary of the Treasury) to utter credit which can be legally monetized. The second way, is through the Congressional affirmation of draft treaties of the U.S. government. A set of leading nations which would enter into relevant treaty-agreements with the U.S. government, would *therefore* constitute the form of the needed fundamental change needed to bring the world rapidly out of the presently onrushing, global breakdown-crisis. The establishing of a network of such treaty-agreements with the U.S., would challenge, and eliminate the present, hyperinflationary, floating-exchange-rate system. A group of nations including the U.S.A., Russia, China, and India, would enable other nations to join as full partners of the new system. That would be sufficient to establish a functioning form of new Bretton Woods monetary system, not in the likeness of the monetarist scheme associated, through policies of the U.S. Truman Administration, with Keynes, but the original 1944 intention of President Franklin Roosevelt.

This would have the moral force of being in service of the Creator's law, and echoes the great 1648 Peace of Westphalia, at a time when the existing, monetarist practice and the promotion of an echo of the Tower of Babel called "Globalization," serves no one as much as the cause of Old Satan.

This poses a series of crucial issues. On that account, we must consider some very relevant history.

The Root of the U.S. Republic

In order to understand anything crucial about modern European history, it is essential that we emphasize, that what became our United States was a product of the direct impact of the stated policy of Cardinal Nicholas of Cusa upon the celebrated Genoese sea-captain in the Portuguese service, Christopher Columbus. Columbus had, since about A.D. 1480, adopted Cusa's mission of reaching across the oceans, as part of a strategy for rescuing European civilization through reaching across the seas to other parts of the planet. Columbus, who committed himself to this mission, approximately A.D. 1480, later, in A.D. 1492, gained the means needed to put that intention, implicit in Cusa's argument, into effect through the support of Spain's Queen Isabella.

On this account, it is to be emphasized, that this same Cardinal Nicholas of Cusa who had prescribed the modern sovereign nation-state system,[9] and also modern science-driven economy,[10] had also set forth the policy of reaching across oceans to outflank the new peril created by the Venetian oligarchy, a policy introduced by Cusa, which inspired sea-captain Christopher Columbus to cross the Atlantic with preceding scientific certainty of the available success of such an enterprise, as aided by scientific knowledge which Columbus had gained by aid of such Cusa associates as Toscanelli.

It is also to be emphasized, that the purpose, and in net effect, the distinction of the process of colonization which led to the creation of the U.S. republic, was to carry the best of European culture to a place which was

---

9. *Concordantia Catholica* (1433).

10. *De Docta Ignorantia* (1440).

Following the intention of the great Cardinal Nicholas of Cusa (right), and of the 1439 ecumenical Council of Florence, to outflank the domination of Europe by the Venetian oligarchy, Columbus (left) was inspired to cross the Atlantic to found a new world, free of such evil influences. The painting (ca. 1460) by Benozzo Gozzoli, depicting the procession of the Three Magi to Jerusalem (in the persons of the Medici), was understood at the time as portraying the arrival of participants to the Council of Florence.

special mission for the settling of what became our United States.

The development of the most successful among the sovereign nation-state republics of the Americas, the United States, has been the leading approximation of Cusa's intention for such a mission. It is this view of the roots of the creation of the U.S. republic, which leads to competent conclusions about the unique accomplishments of the U.S. Constitution; but, it is also the continued reach of the European oligarchy, especially that of the Anglo-Dutch Liberal financier-imperialist interest, which has been the chief cause of every contemptible feature of U.S. history since the rise of the British East India Company's founding of what became the first expression of the imperialism which has been represented by the Anglo-Dutch Liberalism established by Venice's Paolo Sarpi, through to the present day.[11]

a useful distance from the chronic, pro-oligarchical, cultural corruption of "Old Europe," and, thus, to hope, as Cusa had specified, to help bring about the redemption of a corrupted Europe to purposes such as the intentions of the great ecumenical Council of Florence.

Since the time of Columbus' voyages, the leading purpose of the volunteers for trans-Atlantic colonization, was that of taking the best of European culture to a relatively secure distance from the oligarchical forms of corruption which had polluted what were otherwise the best contributions of European culture's science and Classical artistic achievements. All that is good in the U.S.A. since, is chiefly an echo of that sense of a

---

11. The most common folly of most laymen and even professionals today, is the mechanistic presumption that history is the outcome of percussive-like, Cartesian-like, contemporary transactions among individuals. It is the nature of mankind, as distinct from the beasts, that mankind changes its culture, and transmits the impact of those changes down the line of history into relevant future generations. There are few developments in modern European history which do not reflect the powerfully corrupting influence of the "New Venetian" policy and program of the Paolo Sarpi who deliberately created a new center of European imperial power in the northern Atlantic and Baltic regions of rising maritime power, as the way was cleared for this by the disastrous end of the venture of the Spanish Armada. The very idea of Liberalism is a personal creation of Sarpi, who based this policy on the writings of the medieval irrationalist William of Ockham. The way Europeans infected with Liberalism (e.g., empiricism, positivism, etc.) think and act today, especially in the highest ranks of power, is the work of the hand of Sarpi

The crucial fact in this present world crisis is, that the resulting, specific characteristics of the existing U.S. Federal Constitution, provide for a state-controlled system of credit, rather than an inherently usurious, Liberal form of monetary system. This feature of our Constitutional law, makes the U.S.A. the indispensable keystone for the creation of a system of treaty-agreements among sovereigns united for practice by a treaty with a U.S. whose Constitution and past experience, is as under President Franklin Roosevelt. That feature of the U.S. Constitution is uniquely suited, rather then merely expedient, for the work of quickly recreating the needed new, fixed-exchange-rate, international system of credit, which is required for the organization of a global and durable recovery and progress among the physical economies of nations generally.

Here, in these just-stated historical considerations, lies the demonstrably principled authority underlying the intention of both the U.S. 1776 Declaration of Independence and the authority of natural law expressed by the Preamble of the U.S. Federal Constitution,

Founding a New Credit-System

Here so far, I have repeated my emphasis on the distinction between the constitutional credit system of the U.S.A. and the dominant role of monetarist systems in modern Europe thus far. At this point, I carry the discussion of that subject a step further.

As I have already emphasized, earlier here, there are two ways, under U.S. law, for regulating currencies and related international economic treaties.

One, which I have described above, is action of the U.S. Treasury Department's uttering of currency/public credit, by authority of the consent of the U.S. Congress.

The other route, as I have also specified above, is through the consent of the U.S. Congress, to relevant international treaty agreements on international uttering of credit.

Thus, the agreement among a group of responsible nations to a nested set of treaties on credit, tariffs, and trade which involve the U.S.A. as a systemic partner with each and all, is sufficient to create something effi-

ciently tantamount to a "New Bretton Woods." This is the most crucial of the actions expressed as the indispensable role of the U.S.A.'s constitutional system in bringing about an escape from the present brink of a global new dark age.

It must also be recalled that I have emphasized above, that especially under present world conditions, there remains a fundamental difference between the Bretton Woods system prescribed by authority of President Franklin Roosevelt, and the seemingly similar language of the policies of a fixed-exchange-rate system under President Harry S Truman.

President Roosevelt's intention was the use of the physical economic power, for promotion and expansion of that great mass of productive potential which had been assembled for war, for the post-war freeing of the captive peoples of the British and other empires to become truly developing and sovereign nation-states. Roosevelt's foreign economic policy was thus directly opposite to that of both the British Empire and that of President Truman.

The deeply regrettable change, was away from the credit system of Roosevelt's Bretton Woods, to President Truman's support for a virtually Keynesian monetary system. This change, reflected Truman's alliance with Winston Churchill's determination to save the British Empire's colonial and quasi-colonial privileges, privileges which, despite some alteration in forms, persist, essentially, in substantive effect, as intentionally mass-murderously pro-genocidal policies, against most of Africa, for example, especially since such U.S. policy doctrines of the mid-1970s, to the present day. It was U.S. President Truman's adoption of British doctrines directly antagonistic to the constitutional intentions of the U.S.A. which can be regarded, soundly, as the opening for all of the new great catastrophes which have afflicted civilization globally since 1945-46.

The return to the affirmation of our historical mission as a nation, as a renewal of the natural intention of law on which our republic was founded, and as this return was the intention of President Franklin Roosevelt, thus, has, for today, the most extraordinary quality of historical importance at this juncture. Truman rode the train in his 1948 campaign for the Presidency, but pulled up the tracks; we must bring back the railroads and restore the tracks, not just inside the Americas, but world-wide.

The most notable illustration of the need for imme-

---

controlling their minds from the inside still today. All really important thinking today, attacks Liberalism at its actual historical root in the work of Paolo Sarpi.

diate action to this effect, is that the presently accelerating, implicitly hyper-inflationary rate of monetary inflation, is carrying the world as a whole to such a state of chaotic extremity, that reorganization of existing monetary systems as such, would no longer be feasible. In other words, the action which is now urgent, is the chance that we might avoid the already onrushing risk of a chaotic form of a general breakdown-crisis of all of this planet's present monetary systems. Orderly recovery as I am insisting must be done now, as distinct from reconstructing out of chaos, requires that something simply negotiable remains in the existence of a temporarily shrunken, but essential monetary pot of still-viable credit and currency. In this process, we must transform the world's present monetary systems into credit systems. For that, now, time is rapidly running out.

This proposal for action is not to be seen as a utopian's pipe-dream; the world's vital interests now depend upon it, and for now, not some distant point ahead. Its effectiveness depends for its practical success on the included recognition and influence of certain universal physical principles which are virtually unknown to the customary practice and teaching of economics among the governments and economists of today. These are principles which are consistent with what President Franklin Roosevelt did, and are most conveniently approximated from existing records, as the design of the American System of political-economy associated with the United States' first Secretary of the Treasury, Alexander Hamilton, and also with the virtually miraculous application of those principles of the American System under the leadership of President Franklin Roosevelt.

For example, to be extremely practical strategically, if a suitable, viable choice of U.S. Presidential nominee were to come clearly in sight by approximately the beginning of September 2008,[12] when the relevant pre-election nominations had, presumably, been settled, the required prefatory arrangements for the needed form of cooperation among the U.S.A., Russia, China, India, et al., could be put into motion immediately. In that respect, "sooner" could not be "worse." The choice of the next leading U.S. Presidential candidate must be delimited by this strategically crucial consideration; either find and commit ourselves to election of a candidate of those characteristics, or accept the doom of our republic and its people which failure to make such a selection would now virtually assure.

In the meantime during the Summer months, the U.S.A. in particular, and the world in general, will already be, assuredly, plunging ever more deeply into a worsening a state of ruin, a state of ruin which will be far beyond anything imagined by most leading circles of the world as recently as the close of this past May. The sooner the subjective factor of *a promise of a new credit-system's being organized*, the sooner the present dive into a pool of chaos can be prevented pyschologically, and, therefore, the better the chances of avoiding a collapse of even the world at large, a collapse into most extremely calamitous chaos of the planet as a whole.[13] Considering the nature of the onrushing global and other crises of today, we must remind ourselves that qualified leaders of nations must never, as the proponents of he Lisbon Treaty have done, subject a nation to a sense of hopelessness about its own continued existence, especially a very large, and, therefore, very dangerous nation, or its elites, gone mad.

The U.S. Presidency

Consider the uniqueness of what President Franklin Roosevelt accomplished, in breaking the U.S.A. away from London's, Wall Street-pivotted, political control over that control of the U.S. Federal government which had persisted since the assassination of President William McKinley. What Franklin Roosevelt's election accomplished, was a seeming miracle at that time, but it was no accident.

The birth of what became the American System of political-economy, had begun within the pre-1688 Mas-

---

12. Although there is no current evidence that assures us, yet, that one such is about to be chosen. However, we are, indeed, in a time of great, and sudden changes, of one sort or another.

13. As history shows, the possibility of a virtual mass-suicide by the will of the dominant classes, as classes, of an entire nation, or even its reigning elites, is not an impossible event under conditions of extreme crisis. The continuation of the war by the Adolf Hitler regime after the successful allied breakthrough in Normandy, is but one example of this. A large portion of the financier-centered castes of the United Kingdom and the U.S.A. has a clear potential for the "shock and awe" against oneself as the people of a nation, which the Hitler regime was enabled to accomplish temporarily, as it did, through the threat of "unconditional surrender" in the concluding months of that war. So, the fraudulent Versailles charge of "sole war guilt" enabled the British and French governments to create the potential and the threat of the Hitler regime in Germany, and so the "Versailles-like" criminality of the provisions imposed upon Germany under the Maastricht Treaty, imposed with the consent of the U.S. President George H.W. Bush whose father, Prescott, had acted, financially, to bring Hitler into power in Germany.

sachusetts Bay Colony under the leadership of, most notably, the families of the Winthrops and Mathers. It was this "model," typified by the pre-1688 development of the Saugus Iron Works, which was the kernel of inspiration of the young genius Benjamin Franklin himself, his personal development which he contributed to his crucial, personal role in the launching of the so-called "industrial revolution" in England, not the other way around.

Similarly, every regrettable feature of U.S. history has been a reflection of the over-reaching hand of European oligarchism, chiefly that of the Anglo-Dutch Liberal forces of financier oligarchy. The number of U.S. political figures who have accepted honors of British nobility from an imperialist foe of our system, only typifies the hand of corruption reaching into the U.S. political system still today.[14]

So, the intention expressed by the word and practice of President Franklin Roosevelt, as by such as the brave, wise, and good, President Abraham Lincoln before his time,[15] is the fact to which relevant leaders in Russia, China, and India, and other nations, should turn their attention in the matter treated in this present report of mine. The point to be stressed, is not that President Roosevelt did extraordinarily good deeds in his time in office; but that what he did to this effect was nothing different than the intention expressed, in opposition to European oligarchism, in the creation of the U.S. republic.

Particular U.S. Presidents, such as the present incumbent, may have been disgusting, as we have been reminded all too often; but, the intention of the U.S. Constitution itself is a different matter. Admittedly, this leads to certain principled questions, questions which carry our discussion into the heart of the matter of the specific subject of this present report: What is principle, that we might place our faith in its efficacy? What is the principle of such relevant quality in the U.S. Federal Constitution? What, actually, is "economic value"?

II. What Is Economic Value?

In any serious discussion of the history behind the economic policy in Russia today, one must deal with topics expressed in a "special language" which, once spread from Europe into North American settlements, has been customarily used for discussion of the related subject-matters of economic experience and its effects on economic policy-shaping.

This is a "language" which has come to be called "economics," which was originally codified in its present form, by the British Empire, during the course of both the post-1763 decades of the Eighteenth Century and much of the first half of the Nineteenth Century. It is also the language employed by such disciples of the British East India Company's Haileybury School as London-trained Karl Marx. In that respect, the practice of most of what was taught as economics in Britain, as that has been echoed in today's U.S.A., and in the former Soviet Union, was, principally, both an outgrowth of, and, as the case of Marx typifies this, sometimes a reaction against the British East India Company's late-Eighteenth and Nineteenth centuries' Haileybury School.

Even people such as Alexander Hamilton warned, on this account, of the need to take into consideration the language of economy employed by the Anglo-Dutch establishment.[16]

The only significant exception to that program of teaching under the rubric of "economics," in the known history of mankind, has been what is called "The American System of political-economy," as that system is commonly identified with what was uttered by the first Treasury Secretary of the United States, the Alexander Hamilton who was murdered, for related reasons, by the British agent, one-time Vice-President of the

---

14. Relations with a United Kingdom as a republic, would be a different matter than the stench created by the active role of former U.S. Vice-President Al Gore, that of a shameless lackey of the imperial British Royal Household, especially that of a Prince Philip whose avowed intention is to bring about a reduction of the world population to less than one-third the present number of persons, a direction of both intention and deeds done, as shared by Al Gore.

15. Compare the dates of the births of President Franklin Roosevelt and General Douglas MacArthur with the cultural impact upon them of the experience of their parents' and grandparents' generations, especially the effect of the Civil War.

16. The history of the development of the systemically usurious, British school of political-economy is essentially Venetian, starting with the role of Francesco Zorzi (*De Harmonia Mundi*, 1525) in the marriage affairs of England's Henry VIII, through the takeover of the control over the English monarchy of James I by the Venice faction of Paolo Sarpi and such Sarpi agents as Galileo Galilei, as by the school of Rene Descartes and the Paris-based Abbé Antonio Conti. Most notable for the British school of the 1790s and beyond, is the case of Giammaria Ortes, whose 1790 work was plagiarized by the Haileybury School's Thomas Malthus, and who was the actual founder of the modern Malthusianism of such figures as England's Prince Philip and his virtual lackey and former U.S. Vice-President Al Gore. Ortes had a significant influence on Karl Marx's own work in economics, despite Marx's attacks on Malthus otherwise.

U.S.A., and practiced duelist, Aaron Burr.[17]

Such arguments as those put forward in the interest of British imperialism, arguments made in the much-soiled name of economics in our relevant university departments, and other places, today, are based, unfortunately, upon monetarist assumptions, derived from the methods of usury developed by modern Venice on the foundations of medieval banking practices of the mid-Fourteenth Century.

The habits associated with those assumptions and practice, "hedge-fund-like" stealing aside, *have no functional correspondence to any useful, physical-economic function.* However, because of the broad influence of the use of the special language of "economics" used as a rationale for the widespread practices and influence of the British empire, they have supplied many otherwise mutually differing bodies of opinion about economy, with what became a common special language of accounting for discussion among representatives of various proposed theories respecting human economic footprints. The consequent discussion proceeded without discovering the physical principle expressed by the actually walking man. Ordinary economists' practice tells one of certain measurements and certain reportable conditions and events, but tells one virtually nothing of intrinsically physical-scientific interest about *why* an economy behaves as it

The U.S.A.'s first Treasury Secretary, Alexander Hamilton, was murdered by the British agent Aaron Burr, for his role in creating the "American System of political-economy."

does over the medium to short-term intervals, and, with some historical limitations, also long-term ones.

Consequently, as a result of the coopting of Karl Marx by the British Foreign Office, so-called Marxist economics is not only a variety of *British Liberal* economics, as Marx himself often emphasized in describing the fraudulent British utterances of Adam Smith et al. as "the only scientific" economic teaching. This development of that British hoax, in the form this experience impacted the further development of Marx's own political, and general cultural world-outlook, is a teaching which was based, explicitly, on the productions of the British East India Company's Haileybury School.[18]

Although Karl Marx was pulled back by Frederick Engels, in both of these instances, from both what Engels apparently suspected might be Marx's attraction to the influence of the American System economists Friedrich List and, later, Henry C. Carey, Marx caved in to Engels' insistence on a posture of either simply contempt, or hatred toward the American System of political-economy. This is illustrated by study of the case of Engels's frankly silly, so-called

---

17. See Anton Chaitkin, **Treason in America: From Aaron Burr to Averell Harriman** PDF Kindle Epub (New York: New Benjamin Franklin House, 1985), for extensive coverage of the role of Burr. It must be added, that Burr was under the direction of the head of the secret committee of the British Foreign Office, Jeremy Bentham, an utterly depraved creature, as so described by his own published writings; the Bentham who ran key elements of the French Revolution, was also the controller of the Bolivar movement, which was later exposed as a Bentham-directed operation, by Bolivar himself. He was the author of what became known under his personally trained, Foreign Office successor, Lord Palmerston, as the Young Europe organization of Mazzini, and the Young America organization deployed to organize what became the pro-slavery cult known as the London-directed Confederate States of America. Accomplices of Burr included the Andrew Jackson associated both with a treasonous Burr conspiracy and Jackson's position, as an agent of New York banker, author of the Land Panic of 1837 and U.S. President, Martin van Buren.

18. Marx's recruitment involved his assignment to the British Museum under Foreign Office specialist David Urquhart, whose intelligence functions there included his executive role in supervising correspondence among the agents of Palmerston's agent Mazzini. The same foolish Karl Marx who wrote a book "exposing" Lord Palmerston as an alleged "Russian spy," nonetheless knew that he, himself, was an agent of the same Mazzini who would, later, promote Marx, publicly, to head what Mazzini had founded as "The First International." During the period following Palmerston's downfall at the hand of U.S. President Abraham Lincoln, Marx was essentially dumped by the Foreign Office's promotion of anarchism, anarcho-syndicalism, and the French disease known as synarchism (also later known as fascism), and died in relative obscurity as a neglected figure from former times. Marx was later resurrected, in a manner of speaking, by his former associate, Frederick Engels. Engels was to play a significant role on behalf of the Fabian Society, in such projects as the recruitment of the Alexander Helphand, a.k.a "Parvus." This was the Helphand who served as a life-long agent of the Fabian Society in sundry arms-trafficking and other crafts suited to the promotion of what sometime British arms-trafficker and peddler of revolutions, Helphand, would promote as a doctrine of "permanent warfare, permanent revolution:" the fundamental strategic policy of the British Empire's Fabian Society crew of former Prime Minister Tony Blair's time, still today.

Anti-Dühring tract against both Henry C. Carey and Chancellor Bismarck's reforms.[19]

A comparison of sources in British economics, including those which impacted both Marx, directly, and also most of the certifiable Marxist varieties, shows that a common special language is in use for composing descriptions, not only within each variety of brand-label, but among adversarial views of the sort illustrated by both so-called capitalist and Marxian-socialist advocates. This was continued, with some notable exceptions, into approximately the close of World War II, and beyond.[20]

A full break with the early Nineteenth-Century formalities of that special language of economic argument, began with the establishment of the radical-positivist mathematics cults, rooted, inclusively, on the "Malthusian" principle of the Giammaria Ortes admired by Karl Marx. The present-day mathematics cult, was built up, especially since the rise of so-called "systems analysis" during and following the Second World War, around the kernel taken from Bertrand Russell's *Principia Mathematica* and typified by the work of such Russell devotees as Professor Norbert Wiener and John von Neumann.[21]

Therefore, when our attention is focussed on the formalities of Russian economics thinking today, we must proceed with the awareness that we are dealing with the combined effect of the same tradition of the Haileybury School's economic categories employed by Marx and, as this has provided the context within which the decadent faction of Bertrand Russell followers have introduced their von Neumann-style, radical departure from any literate notion of economy. We witness that intrinsically chaotic departure reflected among those Soviet, or ex-Marxist economists found among the devotees of the cult of Cambridge Systems Analysis, as met in Laxenberg, Austria.

So, when discussion turns to post-Soviet Russia today, these diverging traditions, their affinities, their incongruities, and their mutual hostilities, must all be taken into account.

Geometry & Economics

That much said as a matter of defining the context of the subject to be clarified in this chapter. The pivotal point to be considered next, is that there is no scientifically valid, principled notion of a conception of "value" in the economics of either Marx or the Haileybury School.[22]

I mean this in the same sense that there is no true notion of intrinsic physical value in the Sophistry of Aristotle or his follower Euclid, or that of their follower, the hoaxster Claudius Ptolemy. A post-Soviet "ideological" debate on economic matters among these varieties, assumes more the form of a debate among advocates of brand-labels, or parodies on the board-game called "Monopoly," than concern for the substance to which those labels have been sometimes attached by most among today's sundry varieties of economists. Without a credible and powerful adversary to check their power, the London-led international monetarist interest, as echoed by the followers of former U.S. Federal Reserve Chairman Alan Greenspan, had gone utterly, recklessly mad.

---

19. During the last years of his life, Carey steered two most notable foreign projects, one in support of the Meiji Restoration's American System-style economic reforms in Japan, and the other in assisting Chancellor Bismarck in crafting American System-style reforms for Germany. Eugen Dühring was a key intellectual figure among those assembled for the promotion of those Bismarck reforms. In that case, as in Engels' affinity to the conceptions associated with the Thomas Huxley who virtually created H.G. Wells in a laboratory project, Engels' polemics were, essentially, scientifically silly, late-empiricist stuff. During the same period, the great Russian scientist D.I. Mendeleyev was inspired by the Philadelphia Centennial celebration to persuade the Czar to unleash the great new scientific-industrial revolution in Russia of that time.

20. The fact that some economists sometimes produce brilliant insights into physical-economic developments, does not contradict my warnings against generally accepted forms of taught academic and comparable doctrines. The power of insight of creative powers of the individual mind, sometimes leads professional economists to insights which their acceptance of some generally accepted economics doctrines would have never generated. One might wish to say, sometimes: "Yes, he is a brilliant economist, but that is only because he violates the accepted rules for which he gained his status as a trained professional." The case of the late Pobisk Kuznetsov is an appropriate illustration of this point. As an accomplished physicist, he recognized a principle of physical economy, which violated the errant principle of thermodynamics which he defended against the very discovery for which he praised me in economics.

21. The change in conception of economics can be compared usefully with the shift from the positivist view of mechanics, that of Ernst Mach,

---

to Russell's categorical shift, during the same decade, from mechanics, to the standpoint of *Principia Mathematica*. It is worth while to take into consideration the brutish attacks on the work of Max Planck, by the Berlin and Vienna followers of Ernst Mach, during the period of World War I, and the shift to the more radical attack, led by the followers of Bertrand Russell, during the Solvay Conferences of the 1920s.

22. That distinction is expressed as a principled extension of the actuality that there is no actually physical principle to be found in Euclidean geometry, or the practice of financial accounting.

For an example of this type of problem in earlier European history: Aristotle follower Euclid's ***Elements*** is premised upon a set of *a-priori* assumptions, assumptions which are demonstrated, in fact, to have no actual physical-scientific basis.[23] Virtually all of the useful geometry prior to the time of Euclid, had been chiefly derived from astronomy, as this is typified by the case of the *Sphaerics* of the Pythagoreans and Plato. For example: the most crucially systemic demonstration of the difference between the method of science and the method of a-prioristic description, is the celebrated physical construction of the doubling of the cube, as a matter of an actually physical principle of action, by the strategist Archytas, the celebrated Pythagorean of Tarentum, Italy.

In today's world, for example, it is commonplace that students, as in secondary schools and universities, or even as full professors in later life, treat matters of scientific principle as they compose their impromptu opinions concerning works of art. They detach issues of scientific principle from customs of conventional opinions about subject-matters in which they have no systematic involvement emotionally. For them, like Sophists generally, what they wish to be caught believing, praising, or deprecating, is the extent of their emotional engagement in the subject on which they express their "hand-waving" opinions. Like all Sophists, for them, truth is not the issue; being "accepted" by whatever circles by whom one wishes to be accepted, is everything. "MySpace mass-psychosis" is only an extreme expression of that misuse of emotions intended to evade the realities of either physical science, or almost anything else real in life's experience.

What Archytas' constructive form of action, demonstrates, rather than attempts at deductive duplication of the cube, is the same rejection of quadrature of the circle by the principal founder of the modern form of physical science, the Nicholas of Cusa, who pointed out the fallacy of Archimedes' construction of the circle and parabola. Cusa's is the same principle demonstrated for astronomy by Johannes Kepler, and the principle

It was Kepler, and not the fraudster Newton, who made the uniquely original discovery of a universal physical principle of gravitation.

implicit in Pierre de Fermat's principle of least action (against Rene Descartes, et al.), the unique discovery of what is called properly the "ontologically infinitesimal" of Leibniz's discovery of the calculus, or, by Carl F. Gauss' refutation, as in his doctoral dissertation, of the fallacy of the anti-Leibniz hoax of Leonhard Euler, et al., respecting the Fundamental Theorem of Algebra. This is the same principle which underlies the entirety of the work of Riemann, and of the later work of Albert Einstein: all to be considered afresh, as we are obliged to do so in the aftermath of Riemann's presenting of his 1854 habilitation dissertation.[24]

---

23. For example, as I have reported this in earlier locations, my own rejection of Euclidean geometry first occurred on the occasion of my first encounter of this in my secondary school education, when I rejected Euclid on the basis of my observation of the relationship of the physical geometry which optimizes the physical-geometric, dynamic objective of minimum weight and maximal strength of support, which I had previously recognized in my observations made at the Charlestown Navy Yard.

24. Kepler's determination of "equal time, equal area" demonstrates the absence of anything but an ontologically, not spatially, infinitesimal, as a reflection of a universal physical principle of action underlying the phenomenon of gravitation. This notion, as presented by Kepler, was among the two notable challenges by Kepler to "future mathematicians:" the calculus of the infinitesimal (not "infinite series") by Leibniz, and the generalization of the physical notion of elliptical functions by the leading contemporaries of Carl F. Gauss. This same consideration underlies Albert Einstein's view of the work of Kepler, and Einstein's contempt for the systemic fallacy of method expressed by the influence of the followers of Ernst Mach, Bertrand Russell, and Russell's dupes among the representatives of the Cambridge system analysts.

The useful aspect of some of the content of Euclid's work, is located among those principal theorems of his which represent what he had copied from the already established work of predecessors, theorems thus copied and classified as a compendium in the form they are included, with certain bald sophistries added, as features of the **Elements**. The *a-priori* assumptions presented as definitions, have been demonstrated to have been merely arbitrary by their expression of the essential nature of *a-priori* presumptions, and, when they are presumed to be conceptions underlying actual physical principles, are also wrong in the extreme, as the case of the willful hoaxster Claudius Ptolemy illustrates this point.[25]

Much the same is to be said in speaking about what is generally accepted academically as economics today.

A similar folly is demonstrated by the case of the fellow who, when challenged to identify a physical principle, or related conception, goes to the blackboard, or kindred medium, writes out a set of formulations, and then ends his argument with a gesture to which the credulous observers of this performance are intended to respond by uttering "Amen," or: "Q.E.D." The alert member of the audience will then be tempted to respond this ritual by rudely pointing out the obvious: "You did not present an actually crucial *physical* experiment!"

Now, that much said in preparation, what does this mean for the student of economics?

Marxian Economics as Such

You say that you understand Marxist economics. Then, pray tell me what is wrong with it. Why did the Marxists fail? Why did the chosen replacement fail even more badly?

To gain insight into the effect of Marxism on the Russian of today, you must understand the peculiarities of the mind of the present-day American, or the western European, who presumes that he, or she is studying the mental life of today's Russian, when he is actually supplying evidence needed for some crucial, clinical insights into some of the pathologies of his own mental life. Often, amateur and other psychologists, afford us unintended, more and better insight into their own mental disorders than of the mentality of the subjects they pretend to analyze.

Take the illustrative, experimental case of Johannes Kepler's uniquely original discovery of a universal physical principle of gravitation. First, Kepler proves the existence of the Earth orbit as being generated, physically, according to a principle of equal areas, equal times. Since such an actual orbital pathway can not be actually generated by the method of quadrature which had been mistakenly adopted for the circle and parabola by Archimedes, the cause for the orbit can not be located within the confines of the pathway, but the pathway must be regarded as the adumbrated product of the course determined by some universal physical principle which is not directly perceived by the senses, as this fact is qualified in Kepler's development of a general principle of Solar gravitation in his **Harmonies**.[26]

That kind of challenge in the field of physical science, is the same to be recognized in the field of human psychology. It is the principle which adumbrates manifest human behavior which is the truth about human behavior, in the same sense that the planetary orbit is the shadow of the principle of gravitation. This view of psychology is of essential importance in treating mass behavior as culturally directed behavior, as in the mass economic behavior which is our underlying subject of discussion here. The fellow who says, "This is my tradition," or menaces with the assertion, "This is my culture!" or, "This is our culture!" is revealing more about himself, more about the moral defects in his mind-set, than he would wish to recognize.[27]

The fuller meaning of this was shown by Gottfried Leibniz's uniquely original discovery of the calculus, which was done by a unique method derived from close

---

25. For example: all that Kepler says about Aristotle, in the course of his denouncing the hoax by Claudius Ptolemy, must also be said of Euclid's **Elements**. The implications are made clear by the theological attack on Aristotle by the friend of the Christian Apostle Peter, Philo of Alexandria. Contrary to the doctrinal implications of Aristotle, to the theology embedded in Euclid's **Elements**, and to Claudius Ptolemy's fraud, the Creator did not render Himself impotent through the act of Creation. As one dear friend, a celebrated rabbi of our time, insisted: the Messiah will not return according to something like a train-schedule, but when God chooses.

26. As Kepler knew, and warned "future mathematicians," and as mathematicians of Gauss's time showed, there is a qualitative distinction between the ironies of quadrature posed by the generation of the circle, and the higher order associated with elliptical functions.

27. Typical is the "human nature" cant (or, Kant) of the typical middle- to upper-caste Briton. A Classic illustration of this is the argument of de Moivre, D'Alembert, et al., on which they, and others premised the pathological notion of "imaginary numbers."

examination of Kepler's work, and, at a later phase of Leibniz's work, by also considering the relevant implications of the principle of least action traced to Pierre de Fermat: the principle of universal physical least action which Leibniz presented in accord with his collaborator Jean Bernouilli.

The fuller comprehension of this subject-matter was supplied by Albert Einstein's reference to the work of Bernhard Riemann, as showing the relevant deeper implications of Kepler's work for physical science generally, as defining a self-bounded universe, a self-expanding (i.e., *anti-entropic*) universe, which is self-bounded by efficient universal principles akin to Kepler's discovered principle of universal gravitation.

The brilliantly creative Russian physicist Pobisk Kuznetsov, LaRouche writes, "was among the first prominent figures to grasp certain leading implications of my teaching of the principles of physical economy, as opposed to any of the sundry, popularized forms of monetarism." Kuznetsov (center) is shown here with LaRouche in Russia, April 1994.

It is the principle which, thus, defines the formula, rather than the merely stated formula defining the efficiently acting substance, the principle. It is the concept, so defined, which points to the efficiently substantive principle.

There is nothing inherently wrong, in and of itself, in employing a method of description, even if the description as such is not actually sound scientifically. It is by discovering proof of what is wrong about hypothetical assumptions based on such descriptions, that an approach to a scientific treatment of the subject has begun. It is when that distinction of substance from shadow is overlooked, that foolish behavior proceeds.

Therefore, if we treat Marxist economics as a system of description used for a customary, coded practice of financial accounting, without believing it is really a science, it can be used as a convenient way of discussing most of the kinds of matters which, formerly, occupied the attention of most of those university graduates in economics who were serious about using their minds, rather than merely passing grades, or awarding of degrees and titles, who used to be able to understand this point, if only in a Kantian or similar fashion.[28] However, although the Marxist competently trained to behave as a Marxist economist (a rare creature in the world of today) may present an honest and useful description of his intention, yet, he does not know actually why the phenomenon he identifies comes into existence. Where knowledge of principle is lacking, desiring to believe fills the vacuum.[29]

So, in earlier and saner times, before Alan Greenspan, so to speak, the difference between what might be called a theory of Marxist economics and that of any late-Eighteenth-Century or early- through middle-Nineteenth-Century so-called "Classical economist," could be broadly described as a practical difference in meanings between dialects of a common language. (As we used to say that Americans and Britons are separated from one another by the barrier of a common language.) Thus, an economist working for General Electric in the days, prior to the assassination of U.S. President John F. Kennedy, when "fair trade," rather than "free trade," reigned, could conduct exchanges with a Soviet representative, or a German Social-Democrat of the ***Kanalarbeiter*** school, with no particular,

---

28. It should be recognized, that with the present world crisis, such leniency is no longer tolerable.

29. What is often profferred as criticism of Karl Marx's work today, especially since developments of 1989, boils down to the simple observation that, since the fall of Soviet power, Marx ceased to be fashionable.

systemic form of difficulty in understanding the subject-matter which they happened to have under their
common discussion.[30]

Usually, in fact, all three discussion-partners would
have been mistaken, if in differing ways; but, nonetheless, the discussion could be, and often would have
been useful, even, perhaps, productive.

Take my own case as a matter of illustrating this
point.

Although I was attached to the standpoint of Leibniz from middle to late adolescence, and was, if only
implicitly, on the way to what would lead to my adopting Riemann in 1953, the fact is, that during the course
of the post-war interval 1946-1953, as in my professional work as a management consultant, my never
wavering outlook was that of a loyal admirer of Franklin Roosevelt, and as, therefore, implicitly allied, for
patriotic reasons, with the American socialist opponents of President Truman, as against the notorious
Senator Joseph McCarthy, and the Senator and later
President Richard Nixon. My differences as one
among those who could agree with that viewpoint,
never prevented me from understanding, or being understood by any of these varieties of professionals
with whom I had to deal in the course of my practice.
Yet, my own views, especially beginning 1953, were
not consistent in any substantive respect, with any
among those other types. Yet, in a certain degree, on
practical matters of economic analysis and proposals,
in those past times we each tended to express an efficiently practical understanding respecting the subject
under discussion.

Such is life among sensible professional people of
differing persuasions under tolerable circumstances.
Today's circumstances are not tolerable ones. There
comes a time and place when and where such comfort-
able arrangements break down, as now. The prevalent
economic practice by the government of the U.S.A.
today is no longer even tolerably sane, and, in fact, has
not been since the 1970s. Look now at certain among
today's Americans who might imagine themselves to
be looking at today's Russian, while I am actually conducting a clinical assessment of their own behavior and
expressed beliefs.

____

30. The published collaboration between the late John Kenneth Gal-
braith and Professor Stanislas Menshikov is a principled example of
this.

'For the Want of the Nail …'

There is a children's rhyme of some pedagogical
merit, in the poem which traces the loss of a nail in the
horse's shoe, to the loss of that shoe, to the loss of the
horse, and, ultimately, "The Kingdom was lost," all for
the want of a horseshoe nail. The paradox which I have
been outlining here, thus far, partakes of a similar track;
but, this is no children's rhyme. It is the reality of the
situation which confronts the world in economics today.

What is customarily lacking among relevant officials and professionals today, on this account, is the
notion of a physical, rather than financial economy.
That is our "horseshoe nail" in this present discussion.

This lack assumes the form of mass-insanity when
nations consent to the defense of what is termed "a principle of free trade," since advisors of President Richard
Nixon, such as the Chicago School's George Shultz,
(that same which was to give us the neo-Hitlerian Pino-
chet dictatorship in Chile), who had prompted silly
Nixon to scrap the Bretton Woods system which had
been introduced by President Franklin Roosevelt in
1944. The loss of the essential nail of sanity, a post-
1968 loss of cultural sanity, which *a-prioristic* belief in
"free trade" has promoted, is "the loss of that little
thing," the thing taken from us by the same gang, a loss
of an essential principle of competent policy-shaping, a
loss which has been the crucial element of mass-insanity ruling more and more of the world, increasingly,
since that time. This is the trend which has ruled the
international economy of the world, increasingly, producing thus, that step-by-step downward process, since
August 1971, leading into the terminal cancer of the
world-market system today.

To speak of "little things" here, is to say that as long
as money buys what is needed for a person's customary
physical quality of life, the difference between the idea
of a determining physical factor of value, rather than a
value of a monetary process, seems relatively small.
Then, as Russians became acutely aware of a collapse
in a physical standard of life, more than a monetary one,
as under Russia's President Yeltsin, the difference between *physical*, as distinct from money-economy
became no small thing.

For example. in the U.S. until very recently, it was
virtually impossible to convince a typical American that
the U.S. economy had been collapsing physically since
a time no later than 1971-1973 (actually since about
1966-67), when, in fact, that economy had been collaps-

ing at a generally accelerating rate over the entire 1971-2008 interval, and now at a rapidly accelerated rate. The wish to believe the popularized myth, was stronger for the typical individual, than even the increasing painfulness of his, or her own experience of reality.

The crucial factor in this, is the systematic, ideological rejection of that concept of physical economy, the concept on which the brilliant and fertile mind of physicist Pobisk Kuznetsov concurred (largely, at least) with me during the course of our association during much of the 1990s. Comparing this with the trans-Atlantic post-1945 experience, the most destructive factor in the potentially fatal loosening of the nail of physical sanity in economy there, had been the factor of existentialism spread by circles such as those of the followers of Theodor Adorno, Hannah Arendt, et al., under the auspices of the essentially pro-fascist, post-World War II Congress for Cultural Freedom. It is a loss of the sense of the physical production of the means for satisfying physical needs, which is the leading factor in fostering the typical insanity about money met in North America and Europe, an insanity of today which emerged gradually, but then faster, since the aftermath of the 1939-1945 war.

I explain.

The principal immediate victims of the brainwashing of the targets of this cultural warfare, which was directed chiefly against the image of U.S. President Franklin Roosevelt, were chiefly typical members of a so-called "white collar" stratum from among World War II military veterans and their wives, especially those whose careers and aspirations to improved welfare made them extremely sensitive to eligibility for security clearances by the U.S. Federal Bureau of Investigation (FBI) and comparable agencies in the U.S.A. and abroad.

These households were an included target, but the principal target intended was their children, the children of the fear-driven young adults (often the housewife who had not been in military service during the war) of the 1945-1958 interval. It was those children, born to those households, to which the jargon of the 1950s came to refer to as members of families in the social category of "White Collar" and "Organization Man," children born, chiefly, between 1945 and the time of the 1958 depth of a relatively deep U.S. recession. It is those children born during the 1945-1958 interval, who require special attention when we are assessing the most critical of those moral disorders whose

influence on a significant portion of their class, made possible the aftermaths of Spring 1968 in, most emphatically, the Americas and Europe.

The Baby-Boomer Epidemic

The key to the present, middle-aged "Baby Boomer's" mental behavior, is the factor of cultural and also moral depravity embedded, as Sophistry, in the victims of such targeted sons and daughters of the returning veterans from their own childhood in the worlds of the 1930s Depression, the 1939-1945 war, and, then, as the victims of the U.S. Truman Presidency with its threat of nuclear and thermonuclear war, which the Truman administration had launched on London's behalf. It was that experience, which generated what became the hard core of the depravity to be met among a certain sociological nucleus from among those who expressed the special propensity for "purgative violence" in the Americas and Europe, most notably, beginning the Spring of 1968.[31]

There was no significant element of accident in the timing of that 1968er development. Up to a certain point in the course of the mid-1960s U.S. war in Indo-China, educational deferments from induction into active military service had produced a certain indifference to the reality of the ongoing war among those who regarded themselves as the "intellectually privileged," as "draft exempt" representatives of their Baby-Boomer generation.[32] These young people, from among those who saw themselves as privileged, saw the others, of the "lower," "blue collar" social class as those to be considered as suited to serve as cannon-fodder in Southeast Asia, or wherever events might take them.

However, when the call-ups to military service hit the university strata which had enjoyed a self-esteemed

---

31. It is this historical fact which I recognized from studies of subjects such as the early 1930s violent Berlin trolley-car general strike, in my writing and publishing my Summer 1968 report on *The New Left, Local Control, and Fascism*. I emphasized the back-and-forth swapping of memberships from the Communist and Nazi parties during that strike as what I recognized as the crucial bit of clinical evidence of the specifically synarchist feature inherent in the "social chemistry" of the relevant portion of the 1968er generation. This was not, however, spontaneous. The visit of Herbert Marcuse to Columbia University campus during relevant events there, is merely typical of the intellectual manipulation which created the echoes of the Berlin trolley-car strike.

32. Take the illustrative case of current U.S. President George W. Bush, Jr., who escaped combat service during the period of the Vietnam War by the class privilege of assignment to the Texas Air Guard, or, the case of later U.S. Vice-President Al Gore, who avoided military service in a comparable fashion.

Under the reign of Barack Obama- and Howard Dean-funder George Soros, the privileged get the dollars; the others get the "change." Left to right: Soros, Obama, Dean.

privileged class's snickering escape from the threat of overseas military service, as later Vice-President Al Gore had done, fear and hatred of the perceived loss of elitist privilege, combined with the triggers of the March 1, 1968 crisis of the U.S. dollar and "Tet Offensive," became the special detonators of all that was really necessary to detonate the riotous reactions of 1968 and beyond.

If we look more deeply into the minds of those types of 1968er rioters, it was the loss of the credibility of the U.S. dollar, on March 1, 1968 and the effects typified by the "Tet Offensive," which were the crucial detonators, as I saw them during the Spring 1968 developments and beyond. It was not injustice to them which provoked them; what I witnessed was the "existential" fear prompted among those who regarded themselves as representing a privileged idle class, in their flight from their real, existential fear of actually being dumped into the same pot with the types of the combined, "blue collar" industrial and farmer majority whom they came, more and more, to hate.

The spectacle of President Charles de Gaulle, the greatest French hero of the post-war period, being virtually spat upon on the streets of Paris, is a manifestation of the same process expressed in slightly different circumstances. Europe has never recovered culturally, to the present day, from the damage done over the period from the repeatedly attempted assassinations of such as President de Gaulle, the crimes of the assassination of U.S. President John F. Kennedy, and the 1968 assassinations of the Reverend Martin Luther King and Senator Robert Kennedy.

This sociological development of 1968-1971 did not produce the continuing effects which have gripped the U.S.A. and other nations since those times. The kinds of systemic destruction of such pillars of economic and social progress and stability, as that wrecking of the economy and social fabric of our republic continued since President Nixon's folly of 1971 and under the virtual treason of what can be fairly described as the intended, rabid "deconstruction" expressed by the Trilateral Commission during and following the 1977-1981 Carter Administration, have been the drivers of continuing decadence. Such was the intended process of personal and moral deconstruction of selected types of individual figures, chiefly from among the 68ers, who came to embody that synarchist-like immorality of cultural pessimism which has motivated them to destroy every pillar of economic and cultural progress which had been built up in the trans-Atlantic community, and beyond, built up since that 1939-1945 war to defend humanity against what Adolf Hitler had represented.

Any such person who wished to get ahead "in this

establishment journalists' world of things as they are," was likely to have become either a founding member of the 68er phenomenon, or has been, or wished to be recruited to its ranks out of sheer, utterly immoral opportunism, or "for the pleasure of the ride." For many among them, a ride on a share in British agent George Soros' ill-gotten gains, will do, for lack of anything else. Under the reign of Obama and Howard Dean funder Soros, the privileged get the dollars; the others get the "change."

The name of the menace to all civilization today, is thus "the Baby Boomer syndrome," as I have summarily outlined its origins and characteristics here.

It is the hysterical denial of this 1945-2008 history of the "Baby Boomer" syndrome, especially by those of this type now dominating the positions of power in government and the private sector, which is key to understanding the way in which the official U.S.A. mass media, and western and central Europe's Liberal mass media view Russia and Russia's history still today. To understand the motive which makes use of the "Baby Boomer" outlook, we must look to the centers of the power of Anglo-Dutch Liberalism, and participation of those U.S. financier interests in the tradition of the British East India Company's traditional "party of treason" inside the U.S. financier-dominated "Establishment."

Therefore, once we have thus discounted the Baby Boomer factor and the London influence over it, we must ask ourselves: what, really, is economic value? What is the reality of the matter?

III. The Science of Physical Economy

To situate the crucial role of Russia within a "New Bretton Woods" type of agreement under the present, global crisis-conditions, we must look back, most emphatically, to the post-Lord Palmerston characteristics of the setting marked by the combination of the Philadelphia Centennial under U.S. President Grant and the converging U.S.A. relations with Germany, Russia, and Japan (most emphatically). The British monarchy, as an instrument of the neo-Venetian, Anglo-Dutch financier-oligarchical heirs of Paolo Sarpi's legacy, reacted to these relations of the U.S.A. with rage against what these London-centered circles came to label as a grave, "geopolitical" threat.

The most crucial feature of what the British empire regarded as this threat, was the role of U.S. cooperation in, most emphatically, Germany and Russia, in the development of what were intended to become a system of transcontinental railway systems linking the greater part of the continental territory of Europe and Russia in a manner echoing the U.S. development of its transcontinental railway system. Today, that same perceived threat is revived and extended by, most crucially, the scheduled completion of a Bering Straits railway link of the continent of Eurasia with that of the Americas.[33]

Then, the most notable feature of that relationship between the United States and Russia was epitomized by the role of the great D.I. Mendeleyev, who was a crucially important participant in the 1876 Philadelphia Centennial, and the most crucial instrument in forging that scientific-technological development of Russia which was highlighted by, but not restricted to the development of the Trans-Siberian railway.

Through the folly of the Prussian monarchy, over the objections of Chancellor Otto Bismarck, Prussia had continued the war with France after what should have been the primary objective, and conclusion of that war, once the ouster of the British puppet-emperor of France, Napoleon III, by France itself, had been achieved. Thus, through a protected warfare after the proper mission had been accomplished, the Romantically foolish Hohenzollern tribe et al., created an enraged France which would become a British instrument of the *Entente Cordiale*.

Thus, Europe fell into the trap of two so-called World Wars, and such evils as the London-crafted Mussolini and Hitler dictatorships. Thus, in such a manner, Britain, echoing its orchestration of the Seven Years War and the 1763 Peace of Paris, had created the British East India Company's financier-oligarchical empire. Thus, through the foolish Wilhelm II's folly of dumping Bismarck in 1890, Wilhelm embraced the even sillier Habsburg Kaiser in support for that Balkan war which produced the objective, the alliance of Russia against Germany, sought by Wilhelm's uncle, the British Crown Prince Edward Albert (and, later King Edward VII), a development which has kept continental Europe in a state of recurrent destruction since the aftermath of both the dumping of Bismarck and the synarchist style of assassination of France's President Sadi Carnot.

The British imperial intention then, in the immediate

---

33. See Great Projects in **EIR**, May 4, 2007, for proceedings of the April 24, 2007 conference in Moscow on the Bering Strait project.

aftermath of the consolidation of the U.S. victory over Lord Palmerston's Confederacy puppet and the freeing of Mexico from the brutish tyrant Maximilian, was, and remains today, *Britain's geopolitical commitment to the elimination of the threat of a system of truly sovereign, cooperating nations on the continent of Eurasia.*

Today, since 1989, the British imperial objective has included, in addition to attempted financial and political destruction of the U.S.A., the wrecking of the economies of Germany and Russia, and most of continental Europe besides. The included motive is the same: use subversion to ruin the U.S.A. from within, as has been in progress, most notably, since the repeatedly attempted assassinations of France's President Charles de Gaulle, and the actual assassination of President John F. Kennedy: the ruin the already existing and emerging independently sovereign nations of continental Eurasia.

The relevant, contrary, long-ranging, continued strategic interest of our United States, is, as for President Franklin Roosevelt during the course of his life and Presidency during 1939-1945, and remains the promotion of a global system of truly sovereign nation-states, without colonies or semi-colonies, as typified by the U.S. commitment to Germany and Russia from Presidents such as Lincoln and Grant, in the tradition of Secretary of State and President John Quincy Adams. For special reasons, Germany and Russia had special importance for the U.S.A., then, and still, if in a somewhat different form, today.

The fulfilment of that U.S. interest now, requires a shift in the dominant economic policy of the planet, to an alliance among perfectly sovereign credit-systems, away from the kind of monetarist systems which have been deployed from London to cause us to ruin ourselves as we have done so successfully since 1968, and, actually, since the assassination of President John F. Kennedy. The target must include the establishment of a transcontinental railway system which is being upgraded, step by step, from friction-rail, to magnetic-levitation systems operating at speeds in the range of propeller-driven aircraft.

These developments in transportation, which depend largely upon rapid development of nuclear-power systems, are essential to enable nations to develop the extraction and reprocessing of raw materials over extended territories, such as northern Russian Eurasia and Africa, sufficient to support what should be adopted as the common aims of a mankind assembled as a body of respectively sovereign nation-states. For this purpose, Russia represents an extraordinary scientific and cultural potential, both in its territory, and its ability as a scientific power, to develop its territory in ways beyond the present capacity of other nations of Eurasia generally. This development, by Russia, is of crucial strategic importance for all its Eurasian neighbors.

Thus, it is fairly said, from quarters within Asia, that the specific quality of Russia's essential role within Eurasia, and Asia most emphatically, is Russia's role in science. This specific quality of Russia's potential is to be seen as inseparable from the fact that its relevance for today, lies, significantly, in the fact that Russian culture is essentially a Eurasian culture. The practical significance of this for today, points to Soviet Russia's contribution to China's development, prior to the break brought about under the Khrushchev who made a crucial shift not only toward London, but, toward Bertrand Russell. Some of the damage that must have been caused in relations between Russia and China has been repaired. Russia's relations with India are well known. Under present crisis-conditions of the world economy, the prospective relations of China, India, and Russia (and other nations) will be indispensable, not only for all of the nations of East and South Asia, but for organizing a recovery of the economy of the world as a whole.[34]

V.I. Vernadsky and His Age

Long before the work of Russia's Academician V.I. Vernadsky, civilization had already recognized that mankind has experienced three interacting categories of existence: the *pre-biotic*, the *living processes generally*, and *those living processes specific to mankind* which are susceptible of discovery of physical principles, by individual persons, by means of a process through which mankind is enabled to increase the potential relative population-density of our human species, per capita and per square kilometer of the sovereign nation or the planet, as no other known form of life can duplicate this effect. However, there was a lack of

---

34. Take, for example, the keystone role of cooperation among China, Russia, Mongolia, Korea, and Japan. Note, first, the vital strategic-economic interest of Japan and Korea, in their cooperation as a developmental fulcrum of the region as a whole. Thus, it must not be permitted that anything prevent affirmative cooperation among these nations in their common long-term interests, including the importance of frankly protectionist measures for promoting the general development of the entirety of China's territory, that in ways which are prevented by the typically British, imperialist "free trade" policies dominating international trade today.

the concept of the specific scientific principle on which realization of this potential now depends.

With the work of Vernadsky, modern, Twentieth-Century physical chemistry, for the first time, identified the crucially determining distinctions of physical principle among these three categories. Although the development of the exposition needed on this subject is still only a partial one, a mere beginning, some indispensable, preliminary features of those functional distinctions in principle have been settled. Science has been able to show, thus, two fundamental differences of principle which divide existence among three categories: the *abiotic-in-principle, Biosphere-in-principle,* and the *Noösphere.*

Although the mere term "Noösphere" was not, itself, original to the work of Vernadsky; the concept of the *Noösphere* as he defined it, was his uniquely original discovery: it is a demonstrable universal physical principle of modern physical chemistry. A competent physical science of economics, is, therefore, a subject-matter specific to his definition of the *Noösphere.* In the modern history of physical science, that principle is a unique type among the domain of those principles defined, equally, as *both universal, and as the universal's complementary expression as the ontologically infinitesimal:* as this subject was treated, in fact, by those such as Archytas, Plato, Eratosthenes, Nicholas of Cusa, Johannes Kepler, Pierre de Fermat, Gottfried Leibniz, and in Riemannian physical geometry.

The creative principle which defines the uniqueness of the *Noösphere* so defined, is also that principle of the human mind which separates Classical artistic composition and performance from other so-called expressions of art.

Thus, from the vantage-point of this knowledge, the Earth is to be viewed, in functional terms, as composed of these three categorical features, defined such that the

With the work of Russia's Academician V.I. Vernadsky, modern, 20th-Century physical chemistry, for the first time, identified the crucially determining distinctions of physical principle among the three interacting categories: the abiotic-in-principle, Biosphere-in-principle, and the Noösphere.

mass represented by the Biosphere is increasing relative (anti-entropically) to the mass of the Earth as a whole, while the physical mass represented by that higher order of the *Noösphere* (products which are specific to the effect of the processes of the human mind) is increasing (also anti-entropically), relative to that of the *Biosphere.*

Science Is Essentially Personal

Fools propose that science must be "objective." That is a commonplace, but very destructive view of that subject. Science, like Classical artistic composition, is essentially personal, since it is premised upon the creative powers unique to the individual personality. The practice of science in its social expression, must be the interaction among the sovereign creative powers of respective individual, sovereign minds. This social relationship is expressed in the form of one thinker to another: "How did you discover that?"

There are those who argue against this. Their view of so-called "scientific objectivity," belongs more to the department of autopsy than those qualities of mind which distinguish the human creative individual from the beasts, or bestialized individual men and women.

In matters of science and Classical artistic composition, I can not trust anyone, personally, who thinks differently about such matters.

So, for me, my coming to share in this discovery of the Noösphere, was the outcome of my following a decades-long trail, from my adolescent adoption of Leibniz as my principal mentor in study of science then, through my later recognition of Riemannian *dynamics* as being in no way an expression of today's customary use of the term "thermodynamics" by the modern empiricists and positivists; but, rather, as being the outcome of Leibniz's modern contribution to the revival of the science of the ancient Pythagorean and Platonic notions of *dynamis.*

So, for present-day purposes, *dynamic*s has come to be defined implicitly among competent authorities, by the implications of the discoveries by Riemann. This modern view of *dynamics,* as that had been defined by Leibniz, and is to be viewed now from a Riemannian standpoint, has defined my notion of a certain universal physical principle as it is to be expressed in contemporary practice as *a function of potential relative population-density per capita and per square kilometer.*[35]

From the considerations just listed, the notion of a *physical science of economy* is definable for modern civilized practice in broad, but, nonetheless reliable, general terms.

So, for me, it is much better than merely convenient, to examine what I have just written here from the vantage point of what Albert Einstein came to say respecting the combined work of Kepler and Riemann. I must include a repetition of my frequently stated view of modern science, as being what Cardinal Nicholas of Cusa founded, largely by aid from ancient sources, as the modern method now to be traced, as to founding epistemological principles of practice, from Cusa, through Luca Pacioli, Leonardo da Vinci, through their follower Johannes Kepler, and through such as Pierre de Fermat and Gottfried Leibniz.

I have presented the core of this argument itself, in numerous locations published during some previous decades; but, it is essential that it be restated, yet once again, here, as mandatory background, and warning for the reading of what I have to say in this report on urgent issues of economic policy, here and now.

Competent science, such as a competent knowledge and practice of the science of physical economy, and also what is worthy of the name of Classical artistic composition, are like that.

Human knowledge worthy of the names of what are actually the closely related subject-matters of physical science and Classical artistic composition, can not be competently presented as having begun with certain stated, or implied statements of *a-prioristically* "self-evident" presumptions, such as those of the followers of Aristotle and Euclid, or their follower, Claudius Ptolemy. The categorical, systemic distinction of man from beast, and also the related distinction of perception from knowledge, must be our rule.

Mankind is distinguished from all beasts, by our species' manifestation of its unique potential for willfully increasing its own potential relative population-density, as no other living species known to us has been able to manifest this power. Therefore, no competent science, nor truly Classical mode in artistic composition, could be accessed as to principle, except as we refuse to trace the origins of those specific distinctions of human behavior from either the attributable characteristics of beasts, or, as some radical positivists, such as Bertrand Russell devotee John von Neumann, have done: in the worst extreme, from inanimate processes.

Such issues are properly so treated as I do here. Anyone who thinks differently, is lacking something which is essential to the competent practice of a science of economy. The essence of economy is the quality of creativity through which humanity raises the potential relative population-density of the human species, as no lower form of life can do this. That makes the practice of economy truly a very, very, personal responsibility of the individual for his or her contribution to, hopefully, the present and future of all mankind.

Reason versus Sense-Certainty

For a short time, it may appear to some that I am now diverging from the previously stated mission of this report as a whole. Not so. It should be understood that what we are doing at this immediate point, is focusing on identifying a specific conception on which any competent science of economy, *and of the application of that science*, depends absolutely. Like many important discoveries of physical principles of nature, a competent grasp of the way in which economies either actually function over the long span, or do not, often depends upon efficient principles which have been usually ignored, as if they did not exist. Sometimes, as in this case at hand, the matter which has been generally overlooked among professional economists and related scholars, might appear to be a tiny matter in the world at large, but, over the longer term, ignoring it would spell broad and enduring disaster, as the world is expe-

---

35. This has nothing to do with those notions of "thermodynamics" which are associated with the empiricist presumptions of the reductionists Clausius, Grassmann, Kelvin, et al., or the kindred, Machian conceits of Ludwig Boltzmann, et al. The savage attack on Max Planck and his work by the followers of the mystical Ernst Mach during the World War I period in Germany and Austria, and the continuation of this by the followers of Bertrand Russell during the period of the 1920s Solvay conferences, are typical expressions of the sheer nastiness, as much as the epistemological folly of those modern followers of the ancient Olympian Zeus (of Aeschylus' **Prometheus Bound**) who have devoted their professional careers to denying the role of the anti-entropic principle (of "fire") in the discoverable composition of the processes of which the universe is composed.

riencing just such an onrushing, truly global disaster, now.

Therefore, at this point in this report, I place the emphasis on warning my readers of this matter now, at this moment of crisis in human history. I do this since many among them are about to become acquainted, from today's global experience, with consequences which reflect, in a unique and indispensable way, the practical significance of my use of the technical term *ontologically infinitesimal*.

I explain this term with the benefit of an extremely relevant reference to a concept which was introduced by Albert Einstein, concerning the highly personal work of both Johannes Kepler and Bernhard Riemann. Einstein's contribution here, was a concept which he termed that of "a finite, but unbounded" universe, a concept which I prefer to identify as that of "finite and self-bounded" universe, that for reasons which I shall soon make clear here. Einstein's effort was that of one striving to sense the viewpoint of the acting Creator of the universe, with great humility, but with a sense that it was his urgent duty not to misunderstand, not to misrepresent the Creator's viewpoint.

The concept, to which I refer, as Einstein did, is the concept of what Gottfried Leibniz presented as the *infinitesimal* of his calculus. On the latter point, respecting that work of Leibniz, I have already, in various published writings, identified the absurdity of Leonhard Euler's simply fraudulent misrepresentation of Leibniz's use of the term "infinitesimal," a fraud which typifies Euler's part in the mid-Eighteenth-Century attacks on Leibniz's calculus, a fraud which had been introduced by the circles of the Paris-based, Venetian Abbé Antonio Conti, such as Voltaire, Abraham de Moivre, D'Alembert, Euler, et al.

The most appropriate proof in this matter proceeds from the two famous, successive accomplishments by Johannes Kepler in the course of his uniquely original discovery of the universal physical principle of gravitation. I refer to those, again, here: this time for a fresh purpose. The first, the discovery of the characteristic of the Earth's orbiting of the Sun, as in his ***The New Astronomy***, and the second, the development of the general principal of gravitation within the Solar system, in his ***Harmonies***.[36] I limit my account here to the essentials of the matter bearing on the subject-matter of a science of physical economy. I frequently repeat myself in the following summary, that for reasons which should require no explanation.

The unique quality of beauty of his mind in those and related works, is that he grasps the essence of the point I have just emphasized above: competent science, when its subject is the role of human creativity within it, is intensely personal. This is outstanding in Kepler's work, pronounced in Leibniz, concealed, but resonant, in the work of Gauss, opens up again with Bernhard Riemann, and gains loving expression again in the reflections of Albert Einstein during the last four decades of his life.

After all, anything which bears upon the uniqueness of the aroused creative powers of the individual human mind, promotes the soul to shout "Eureka!" in one way or another, and is expressed with an intensified moment of playfulness of a certain free-spirited kind, or it is not creative at all. Science and art are not for grim gravediggers.

Thus, in the first instance, once Kepler had gone through the successive steps by which he crafted his work showing the Earth's elliptical orbiting of the Sun, in ***The New Astronomy***, his measurements showed that this orbit was ordered by a principle of action whose effect he described as "equal areas, equal times." *This evidence already demonstrated, in itself, the absurdity of the presumption that the orbit could have been determined by an ordering of that elliptical pathway which is congruent with Archimedes' mistaken quadrature of the circle.*[37] This, by itself, exposed the virtually childish absurdity of Euler's joining the previously stated, silly argument (for the "imaginary") copied from de Moivre's and D'Alembert's specious attack on the infinitesimal of the Leibniz calculus (as "imaginary").

This set of considerations leads, in the second instance, from that point, through the development of the general measurement for gravitation within the Solar System, to the notion which Leibniz was to define later, as the role of *the ontologically infinitesimal*, rather than *a simply geometrical infinitesimal*, a notion which Leibniz crafted in accord with the prompting from the work of Kepler. The measurement of the crucial phenomena, in this matter, requires two measurements, one

---

36. See the LaRouche Youth Movement documentation of its team's reliving of the process of these discoveries by Kepler.

37. The discovery of the calculus and the exploration of physical functions of an elliptical form, were two tasks which Kepler had referred to the work of future mathematicians. The first was solved by Leibniz; the second, among Gauss and his relevant contemporaries.

according to the principle of *the sense of* sight, the second according to what Max Planck implicitly emphasized, contrary to the apostles of Ernst Mach, and contrary to the devotees of Bertrand Russell later, as the systemically contrary notion of dynamics expressed by the function of hearing, rather than mechanics.[38]

The two measurements, combined, created an image in the mind of Kepler and other scientists, like the argument by Fermat and by Leibniz, both of whom followed Kepler in this method: an image-like conception entirely outside the domain of naive sense-perception as such. In this way, Kepler, as a follower of Nicholas of Cusa, took any competent science after him entirely out of the domain of Euclidean *a-prioristic* presumptions, rightly downgrading sense-perception to the status of instrument-readings, rather than naive sense-certainties. By adopting the systemically, mutually contradictory "instrument-readings" of sight and musical sound, a reading of the evidence, by Kepler, which made ridiculous the later effort by many to substitute Titius-Bode for Kepler's own work on the organization of the planetary orbits.

The still deeper implications were made clearer by Einstein's presentation of the argument, such that when we introduce the relevance of Bernhard Riemann's work for its bearing on the work of Kepler and Kepler's legacy, it becomes clear that, in terms of demonstrable universal physical principles, our universe is intrinsically *finite and self-bounded* by principles such as the uniquely original discovery, by Kepler, of the role of gravitation in the organization of the Solar System.

How could that which is universal become "visible" to the senses, except as it changes? Did the Creator render Himself impotent by Creation of a universe? If the change is not anti-entropic, then it may be made visible, if only to memory, in terms of the change to becoming less than before; but, otherwise, it can be made visible only if the change was to something which never was before, as if the universe were ordered anti-entropically, as a finite, self-developing universe, an expanding process of continuing, universal creation.

The latter quality of change to a higher order of existence, is a definition of creativity (i.e., anti-entropy), such as human scientific creativity in discovery of universal physical principles, and their applications, an action of discovery on which increase of the potential

relative population-density of a culture depends in practice.

The fact is, that a discovery, such as Kepler's uniquely original discovery of universal gravitation, could be made only by a sovereign individual mind, an experience which can be made known by others in no way but as the replication of the process of an experimentally demonstrable discovery by another individual mind. This notion of an individual human person's creativity, is the key for unlocking the door to the apparent mystery of the Leibniz *ontological infinitesimal*. This leads us to unlocking the apparent mysteries of the Biosphere and Noösphere. This leads us to what some might otherwise regard as the mystery of the science of physical economy.

How Man Sees His Universe

What, then, is the required design of an experiment, which shows the way in which human creativity can be demonstrated, not only as an efficient source of increase of human potential relative population-density, per capita and per square kilometer of the Earth's surface, but as creativity has just been defined in our progress in this report thus far?

For this purpose, let us, first, take the case of qualitative steps of incremental process sometimes named an increase of what has been termed, since the closing decades of our preceding century, as "energy-flux density," as stepwise progress from burning of wood, charcoal, coal, coke, nuclear fission, and thermonuclear fusion, typifies a case of a prompting of qualitative leaps in potential human productivity, as per capita and per square centimeter cross-section of the ongoing energetic process.

The problem which this conception presents for some scientifically trained specialists, lies in their conditioned adherence to a reductionist, virtually Cartesian misconception of physical scientific principles: the misconception associated with the notion of particles which happen to be in motion, for what should be the obvious reality, that nothing exists except as if it were in motion.

The general principle of progress, is that a discovery of a valid universal principle, leads to applications which increase the productivity of mankind by *a significantly greater amount of net gain* than the cost incurred by the discovery and investment in its application. This leads to a relevant increase in capital-intensity, both of the investment itself, and in the course of its use; but, the gain realized, when these investments are

---

38. See Bernhard Riemann, "Mechanik des Ohres," **Werke,** pp. 339-359.

properly applied, is, and must be, rather soon, greater than the sum total of the combined direct, and indirect costs of the investment itself.

This is *a physical concept* of an act of creativity, a concept which, for reasons just stated, could not be competently represented functionally in terms of ordinary financial accounting, nor by any Cartesian, or kindred methods, nor stated in terms of existing financial systems or prevalent economic dogma.

In the first approximation, but only first approximation, we should consider only the increase in energy-flux density of the source of power supplied to the process, for, in this case, in first approximation, the assumption that the process is not changed otherwise.

To express this quality of effect in another way: as "any increase in productivity obtained at a physical cost which is, after the fact, in principle, less, in net effects, than the physical cost of making and maintaining that change."

Let us now combine the two notions just presented under the rubric of "cases of benefits derived from increases in capital intensity."

Now, combine the two, as combined increases in energy-flux density with the margins of benefit derived, in the same case, from general increases in capital intensity.

Let us add another qualifying consideration. So far, we have considered benefits expressed in the form of inputs to the productive, or comparable process. Now, let us include all margins of quantifiable benefit afforded to the consumer by means which require increasing the capital-intensity of the productive, or related process.

Now, gather these and related kinds of parameters within the dynamic process of an appropriate Riemannian manifold. Consider the following, "rule of thumb" form of descriptions.

Then, map the process so outlined for those aspects which are products of changes which had been made, from some earlier dynamic state, an outcome which were effected through applied discoveries of universal physical principle.

Now, consider another track. Consider some relatively simple illustrations.

Normalize the rate of solar radiation impinging on the planet; employ a normalized spectrum. Do this for the purpose of defining a standard scale of physical-economic reference for human life on Earth.

Consider solar radiation and water. How is the rela-

tionship between the two to be enhanced? Now consider moving large masses of water about, to increase the "green cover" of the planet's surface, thus increasing the biomass of regions of the planet per capita and per square kilometer, and producing a moderating effect on weather-patterns, and increasing the relevant biomass, rather than merely heating up the atmosphere by not taking such measures. Combine this with the increased development of supply and development of sources of controlled power of generally increased energy-flux density. *(Never commit the wicked prank of degrading a product of living processes, generally, as by reliance on so-called "bio-fuels," into the contrary direction of transforming living processes into dead ones. The goals of economy in our Noösphere, must be the triumph of life, especially human life, over non-life, and of the creative powers of the human being, over the bestial.)*

Now, consider combining the benefits of increase of energy-flux density, with the adjustment of the relationship between use of impinging Solar radiation and water resources, to enhance green cover.[39]

In all of these illustrative images which I have just presented, there is a commonly underlying coherence with the same principle of discovery of universal physical principles which is illustrated by the referenced case of Kepler's discoveries. Moreover, all competent discovery is, in its net effect, coherent with that principle of (for example) modern European science introduced by Nicholas of Cusa and reflected in what I have described as typical of the discoveries of Kepler. All of the illustrations I have just written here converge on a Riemannian quality of manifold, not a Euclidean, nor Cartesian, nor any other reductionist method.

The immediately preceding points of illustration bring us to the matter of the relevant systemic errors, over about a century and a half, of the so-called "orthodox" Marxist economists. The problem to be considered is lodged in the intrinsically reductionist fallacy of the so-called "labor theory of value," a fallacy which Karl Marx derived, chiefly, from the British environment in which his systematic views on modern economic processes were shaped by Urquhart and the circles of the Haileybury School tradition, that during about two decades of Marx's life there.

It was this same flaw, which Marx came to share

---

39. Including margins of quantifiable benefit afforded the consumer by means which require increasing the capital-intensity of the productive, or related process.

with the Haileybury School whose works he studied, which was employed by the marginal utilitarians as a pretext for the utter nonsense which they produced. It was a relatively short step from the marginal utilitarians, to the Romantic follies of the positivist Ernst Mach, and, then, to the utter lunacy of the followers of Bertrand Russell, such as Norbert Wiener, John von Neumann, and their devotees of today, such as the forecasters in the likeness of the LTCM of 1998 notoriety.

It is the creative powers of the individual human mind which generate all the true increase in wealth produced by mankind, that in mankind's essential physical expression as the Noösphere. These are the same creative powers, expressed by the work of such as Kepler and Leibniz, expressed by physical science in that tradition. These are also expressed in what may be identified as the "social theory" which is the implicitly governing principle of strictly Classical modes of artistic creativity, as the latter influence was identified by Percy B. Shelley in his **In Defence of Poetry**: the increase of "the power of imparting profound and impassioned conceptions of man and nature." There is no true science, nor true Classical art without such artistic passion.

So much as a matter of broadly stated introduction to what we must now address as the kernel of the matter.

The Noëtic Principle

The considerations which I have sought to illustrate roughly by aid of the preceding illustrations of a point about the principles of physical economy, all converge on two interdependent facts about the individual member of the human species, facts which each bear implicitly upon V.I. Vernadsky's Riemannian, physical-chemical definition of the Noösphere. First, that no animal species known, is capable of that function of creativity which is typical of the distinction of the human species from all others. Second, although creativity can be echoed, as if broadcast, from one human mind to another, all acts of creativity occur only within the sovereign powers of the relevant individual mind. We can, and must stimulate the creative activity of the other's mind; but, there are no available, "wired connections."

Both considerations force attention to the fact that, contrary to modern Sophists such as Clausius, Grassmann, Kelvin, Boltzmann, et al., entropy is not a law of the universe; the universe is *intrinsically anti-entropic*: e.g., *creative*.

Yet, paradoxically, the manifest human creative function is located as an activity associated with the individual human brain, although no known animal brain has been discovered to be capable of species-anti-entropic creative powers. Yet, the development of the Solar System from an isolated "young Sun," is a reflection of a creative process. The suggested implication is, that the universe as a whole is creative, but many of its products are not creative when the relevant experiment is designed, by use of a fallacy of composition, as in and of itself, in a reductionist mode, rather than a truly dynamic one. The increase of the relative mass of the Earth's Noösphere, relative to the Biosphere, and the Biosphere relative to the abiotic portion of the matter, calls our attention to such matters.

This is a matter which I have addressed, sometimes at significant length, earlier.[40] I recapitulate some relevant essentials here. Science is history, and history is also science. For an example of this we have the following.

A History of Imperialism

We know, that the currently prevalent dogma of taught thermodynamics, is a reflection of the same ancient oligarchical principle portrayed in the famous **Prometheus Bound** of Aeschylus.

What Aeschylus portrayed, thus, is otherwise known in ancient through modern European and West Asian tradition as *the oligarchical principle*. The known origin of that tradition is traced back to as far as ancient Babylon and its priesthood. It was continued beyond the fall of the power of Babylon by the Babylonian priesthood's role in other Asian dynastic systems, and was the proposal for a two-empire, Asian and European system, during the period following the collapse of Athens in the aftermath of the Peloponnesian War. The essential distinction between the two, was that the Asian version was derived, at least proximately, from what had become a land-based culture, whereas the western part, such as that of ancient Egypt,[41] was based, directly, on a Mediterranean-centered maritime culture. The British empire, for example, is an offshoot of successive evolutions of the western mode in empire, beginning with the Roman Empire established by that

---

40. Cf. Lyndon H. LaRouche, Jr., "Vernadsky & Dirichlet's Principle," *EIR*, June 3, 2005.

41. Contrary to the foolish fad of an "hydraulic" society, civilization, as in the case of Egypt, moved upstream, from the oceans, not downstream. Astronomy as a product of transoceanic navigation and related developments, attests to this.

pact, struck on the Isle of Capri, between Augustus Caesar and the priests of the cult of Mithra.

The imperial model, otherwise best identified as the oligarchical model, is premised on the intention of preventing the natural creative powers of the human individual from coming to fruit in such a fashion that what might be termed "the lower classes of society" might not continue to submit to the overlordship of a ruling class. In other words, the Olympian model of oligarchy which is presented as the principle of evil in Aeschylus' ***Prometheus Bound***.

In the oligarchical model, as from the founding of the Roman Empire through the Anglo-Dutch Liberal fiancier oligarchy of today, the general population of society, and of the societies ruled by an imperial tradition (e.g., the Olympus of ***Prometheus Bound***), is "managed" *through maintaining pro-genocidal limits on the growth of the general population*, opposing scientific and technological progress, by vulgarizing popular culture, and by preventing knowledge of the actual universal principles on which mankind's rule over nature depends: in short, the evil, progenocidal, neo-malthusian policies of the Hitler regime and of the World Wildlife Fund of Britain's Prince Philip and his lackey, former U.S. Vice-President Al Gore.

The new form of empire which emerged from the leadership of Venice's Paolo Sarpi (above) spawned today's Anglo-Dutch Liberal system, and unleashed the swarm of financiers at its core; the imperialist speculators in today's petroleum "spot market" are the direct heirs of Sarpi's model.

In modern European society, this legacy of the mythical Olympian Zeus, means a policy of limiting knowledge of scientific principles to a small, tightly controlled scientific elite, which is usually of the intellectually castrated variety, thus incapable of expressing genuine, carnal knowledge of the role of universal principles in science, but, chiefly, only mathematical formulas as substitutes for reality.

The most significant modern expression of that kind of oligarchical rule, is what is most accurately identified as the Anglo-Dutch Liberalism institutionalized through the "New Venice" faction of Paolo Sarpi. The distinction of Sarpi may be fairly summed up by stating that the most essential of the keys to Sarpi's reforms, is that he dumped the Aristotle whose barren doctrines had been the principal method of oligarchical "brain-washing" of European culture in earlier times, as replaced by the new form of oligarchical brain-washing, called Anglo-Dutch Liberalism, the so-called Liberal philosophy launched by Sarpi, and based on the medieval irrationalism of the William of Ockham whose lunacy is the central feature of modern logical-positivist dogmas.

The new form of empire which emerged from the leadership of Paolo Sarpi, is what is called the Anglo-Dutch Liberal model. This Anglo-Dutch Liberal model is based on the ruling authority of an otherwise anarchic class of financiers in the tradition of Venetian usury, neo-Venetian usurers following the Liberal traditions of Sarpi. Sarpi launched that swarm of financiers who constitute the essential core of the imperial power of the present Anglo-Dutch Liberal imperialism nominally centered in London, as expressed typically in the imperial power of the post-1973 petroleum "spot market."

The leading opponent of that form of Anglo-Dutch Liberal imperialism which assumed the form of an imperial power of the then British East India Company, with the 1763 Peace of Paris, was the American faction generated, chiefly, by such leaders of the Seventeenth-Century, English American colonies as the Massachusetts Bay Colony of the Winthrops, Mathers, and their principal intellectual heir, Benjamin Franklin.

Through that relative isolation of the young United States constitutional republic from its former European friends and sympathizers, which began with the British Foreign Office's orchestration of the siege of the Bastille by "Philippe Egalité," the Jacobin Terror, and tyranny of Napoleon Bonaparte, the U.S. emerged from the effects of the 1814-1815 Congress of Vienna as largely an isolated and embattled republic. This relative isolation was continued until it was broken by the victory of the U.S. over the combined British, French and Spanish forces deployed against the U.S.A. and Mexico by Lord Palmerston's British Empire, together with London's creature the treasonous Confederate States of America, against both the U.S.A. and Mexico.

Since the U.S. victory over Palmerston's efforts, world history has centered around the continued conflict between two leading English-speaking powers, the United States against the British Empire of Anglo-Dutch Liberal interests in the cultural and political, imperial "free trade" tradition of the financier-oligarchical Liberalism of Paolo Sarpi.

Since then, all other politics of the world since the occasion of the February 1763 Peace of Paris, have pivoted upon a dependency on the issues separating the two leading groups of English-speaking powers, the U.S.A. versus Anglo-Dutch financier-imperial Liberalism. This balance of power between the two leading, English-speaking powers, has been not only a conflict between two territories in the world; it has also been a conflict between the patriots and Liberal Tories within the United States. An Anglo-Dutch Liberal hatred of the kind of prosperity ensured by the global influence of the American System of political-economy.

However, do not forget, that the actual happiness of the British Isles' "normal people" was not a pleasing prospect for a royal financier oligarchy in the tradition of Venice's Paolo Sarpi and his northern European maritime region's ambitious followers of Sarpi's "New Venice" policy.

Truman, Unfortunately

This depraved, pro-oligarchical intention by President Truman to which I referred above, was spoiled by the Soviet Union's unexpectedly early development of a nuclear-weapons capability, a development which spoiled the publicly declared intention by British imperialism's Bertrand Russell to launch a so-called "preventive" nuclear assault on the Soviet Union, on the assumption the Soviet Union would not possess a military-nuclear capability at that time.[42] This cleared the way for the election of the immensely popular General Dwight Eisenhower, who delivered significant setbacks to the British war-hawks and their U.S. likenesses.

However, after Stalin's death, his successor, Nikita Khrushchev, entered into an arrangement with the British circles of the same Bertrand Russell who had echoed the policies of Russell's deceased political confederate, "futurologist" H.G. Wells, with Russell's own, earlier nuclear saber-rattling.[43] Khrushchev's launching of the "Cuba missiles-crisis" was an integral feature of the same operation which launched repeated assassination-attempts against France's President Charles de Gaulle and others during the span of the 1961-1968 interval, including that of President John F. Kennedy. The launching of the U.S. fraudulently launched war in Indo-China and the 1967-1968 monetary crisis triggered by Britain's Prime Minister at that time, ended the continued influence of the policies of real physical-economic growth which had still been U.S. policy over the post-Franklin Roosevelt, 1945-1967 interval.

The emblematic, strategic features of this time were the continuation of the Indo-China war, the economically counter-revolutionary rampage of the "anti-blue collar" 68ers, and the break-up of the Bretton Woods agreements by the administration of pro-fascist President Richard Nixon. The British-Saudi orchestration of the oil-shortage hoax of the 1970s, which established the Anglo-Dutch "spot market" as a virtual replacement for the earlier pace-setting role of the U.S. dollar, when combined with the Trilateral Commission-steered destruction of the essential features of the U.S. physical economy, wrecked the U.S.A., and cleared the way for what has become the post-1987, inflationary destruction of the U.S. dollar and, later of its associated physical economy under the incumbency of U.S. Federal Reserve Chairman Alan Greenspan.

The result of this trend in the rise of Anglo-Dutch Liberal power, at the expense of, most notably, an in-

---

42. The significance of this Soviet development of nuclear weapons, is not properly recognized until it is noted that the Soviet development of an Anglo-American mode in such weaponry was, reportedly, the result of Stalin's decision to test a U.S.-like type, rather than the already developed Soviet type, so that a failure of the test could be blamed on a flaw in the copying of the U.S. type, rather than the Soviet type.

43. The sometime avowed fascist, H.G. Wells of *The Open Conspiracy* and *Things to Come*, and of the H.G. Wells Society loose inside today's U.S.A., was originally a youthful protege of the nasty Thomas Huxley of sundry Nineteenth-Century notorieties and. later a leader of the followers of Cecil Rhodes in preparing the way for launching of what became known as World War I. It was the death of Wells which bequeathed to Russell the authorship of the fascist, post-World War II scheme for a "preventive" nuclear-weapons attack on the Soviet Union, that for the purpose of establishing "world government." Russell gave up the advocacy of such a nuclear assault on the U.S.S.R., when it was discovered that the Soviet Union had also developed a nuclear-weapons capability of its own.

creasingly ruined U.S. economy, has been a resurgence of nothing other than the old British Empire in unwashed, but newly pressed old rags of a past imperial glory. This is a development better described as resurgence of the power of Anglo-Dutch Liberal financier interests, that now in a form echoing the Fourteenth-Century conditions and trends leading into the "New Dark Age" of Europe's Fourteenth Century.

Sometimes, even sophisticated people are astonished by my insistence, that the only true empire of the world today is the Anglo-Dutch Liberal empire set into motion, as the new model of Venetian empire, by Paolo Sarpi. That astonishment reflects a lack of sufficient attention to the true distinction of human beings from the beasts. I explain this extraordinarily important point.

The Effects of Cultural Stagnation

The crucial point is the distinction of the Noösphere from the Biosphere. The aspect of this distinction on which to focus at this point in the report, is the fact that lower species of life have relatively fixed levels of potential relative population-density, relative to their environment and its current condition; whereas, the cognitive powers unique to the human species, are the source of a voluntary power of the human species, a power to change its potential relative population-density, upward, as no other species can do this. This reflects a specific power of the human mind which does not exist in the animal brain.

Thus, speaking strictly, although mankind can attribute a history to the existence of an animal species, no animal species can attribute such a voluntary history to itself. Man is thus fairly described as a distinctly historical species.

Thus, patterns of principled kinds of policies transmitted over successive generations, act like the *a-priori* forms of axioms and postulates attributed to a formal geometry, to such effect that seeming traditions of a certain society during a certain time impose what are effectively ideas generated in the past, acting upon several of more, successive, later generations. In that specific sense, the very wicked Mr. Paolo Sarpi is very much alive, as a willful agency today; only his human body is dead.

This fact of historical man, as distinct from animal species, has been the principal source of my uniquely successful history as a long-range forecaster over more than four decades. That is to say, that day to day decisions, even innovations, have only a very limited influence over history in the longer term, for as long as certain relevant, principled types of policies, policies of a type which characterize a cultural mind-set, remain in effect. Other kinds of decisions have only a relatively minor, temporary effect in shaping the direction of a society's movement into its future. The principal, axiomatic-like assumptions of belief associated with the existing social system prevail, until some breakdown or equivalent change in the course of history intervenes to change the course of history.

Thus, to understand the Anglo-Dutch Liberal system of imperial tyranny which menaces world civilization today, you must understand that the legacy of Paolo Sarpi still reigns. Think of adopted "axioms," such as the arbitrary axiom of "free trade," as akin, in its functional effect on human behavior, to genetics in the design of an animal species. The imperialist Liberals of today are, as a social class, a species with the "genetic" characteristics transmitted from Paolo Sarpi. To understand them, you must first study the case of their "genetic" ancestor, one like the Grand Inquisitor of Dostoyevsky's novel, the evil, virtually Satanic, Paolo Sarpi.

The Choice Before Nations

Thus, the only competent economic policy of any nation, or for the world as a whole, is what is loosely described as a "science-driver" policy for both sovereign nations and the world community at large. All of the principal evils known as the cause for failure of nations and peoples, are expressions of either a neglect of that policy, or, worse, commitment to uproot it, such as that of modern Malthusians from Malthus through genocidalists such as Adolf Hitler's regime, or today's former Vice-President Al Gore today.

Thus, the efforts to defend humanity from brutish systems of government and conventions, during the interval from the accession of William of Orange to power in England, as the virus which was the cultural legacy of Paolo Sarpi's neo-Venetian Liberalism, settled upon its new geographical, Anglo-Dutch nesting-places, and consolidated the outcome of this as the habit more or less securely established in most of Europe by the post-Seven Years War, February 1763 Peace of Paris.

There had been several qualitative steps leading into this and ensuing results since the cultural disaster of the expulsion of the Jews from Spain by the Grand Inquisitor, Tomas de Torquemada, acting in concert with the takeover of the Spanish monarchy by the Habsburg in-

Belief in Newton, writes LaRouche, "is a matter of pagan religious belief, not science. The cult of Isaac Newton can be traced chiefly to Sarpi's lackey Galileo (left), who produced a series of hoaxes which became his alleged scientific accomplishments. The engraving is titled, "Newton's dog burns his Alchemy writings in 1693."

terest. The impact of a subsequent, parallel change from the reign of Henry VII to Henry VIII in England, engineered by leading Venetian intelligence official and impromptu marriage-counsellor to Henry VIII Francesco Zorzi, had been a keystone for a plague of religious warfare in Europe which persisted as a trend from 1492 until those actions of Cardinal Mazarin which triggered the 1648 Peace of Westphalia.[44]

In the midst of this 1492-1648 interval, Paolo Sarpi had risen to prominence as the leader of a faction of reform for a significant portion of the Venetian oligarchy. This did not mean that Sarpi was devoted to a peace of faiths; the best evidence is that he sought what became, in effect, the Thirty Years War of 1618-1648. Sarpi was not motivated by desire for peace; his concern was the inability of Venice, under its pre-existing social policies, to suppress the political-economic legacy of such as Nicholas of Cusa, Louis XI's France, and England's Henry VII. The economic, scientific, and social reforms unleashed by Cusa et al. in the great ecumenical Council of Florence, had produced a science-oriented, urban, city-centered culture, which the massed forces of the Habsburg interests could not suppress as long as they clung to radically Olympian, Aristotelean dogma respecting social-technological practice.[45]

Sarpi's policy was one of seeking to maintain Venice's power as a finance-imperialist interest, by adapting to, and working to corrupt the scientific-technical changes in European culture, rather than fighting against them. Therefore, the keystone of Sarpi's policy had been what is known today as Anglo-Dutch Liberalism. For this, Sarpi needed an ideological lever, which he found in his revival of the irrationalist ideology of a notorious medieval figure, William of Ockham. This substitution of Ockham for Aristotle, by Sarpi and Sarpi's lackey Galileo, and Sarpi follower Thomas Hobbes, became the core of the Anglo-Dutch Liberal dogma adopted and spread by the emerging Anglo-Dutch imperialism of the Netherlands and Britain. The case of the virtual "stuffed dummy," of the circles of Antonio Conti and Robert Hooke, Isaac Newton, is the typification of the philosophical world-outlook of a modern British culture embodying the living spirit which had occupied the former mortal figure of Sarpi.[46]

---

44. Mazarin had been the Papacy's chief agent in the efforts to bring about peace between France and Spain. He continued that assigned function with his movement into France, where he succeeded the authority held by Cardinal Richelieu.

45. Consider the opinion of a close friend of the martyred Christian Apostle Peter, the Jewish rabbi Philo of Alexandria, against the doctrine attributed to Aristotle. Aristotle had defined a God rendered impotent by the attributed "perfection" of his Creation, thus leaving Satan free to roam. The point is, that what was created was an anti-entropic, inherently creative universe. The argument against which Philo, among Christians and others, complained is to be recognized as that of the evil Olympian Zeus of Aeschylus' **Prometheus Bound**, the satanic Zeus on whom the worship of Malthus and Prince Philip's batty World Wildlife Fund is premised.

46. Whereas, the actual and unique establishment of the calculus had been published by Gottfried Leibniz, before his leaving Paris, in 1676, the later claims of Isaac Newton's keepers rested upon the claim that Newton had already made the discovery, but had neglected to publish it. The explanation proffered by the keepers of the Newton cult, was that the original discovery was to be found in Newton's chest of scientific papers, which, it was explained, had been mysteriously misplaced. Said chest finally appeared in the Twentieth Century. The celebrated John Maynard Keynes was entrusted with examining the contents. A Keynes horrified by the mass of black magic and similar materials contained within the chest, proposed publicly that it be shut tight, and never opened again. In fact, no actual calculus was ever produced by Newton, or in Newton's name, during his lifetime; what was produced was a

What Was Isaac Newton?

The origin of what became the cult of Isaac Newton, is traced chiefly to Sarpi's lackey Galileo, who used his access to some of Kepler's work through Kepler's correspondence on music with Galileo's father. Galileo, in his other role as Sarpi's ideological lackey, produced a series of hoaxes which became his alleged accomplishments in science. Later, Galileo's model was employed by his English followers to copy and reify relevant published writings by Kepler, to fabricate a mangled and fraudulent attribution of the discovery of gravitation to a science-incompetent figurehead, Isaac "Open the Window" Newton.[47]

In short, belief in Newton is a matter of pagan religious belief, not science. The god of that particular pagan religious cult, was not God, but something tantamount to the Olympian Zeus of Aeschylus' *Prometheus Bound,* a pagan god whose traditional priesthood came to include the plagiarist and hoaxster Thomas Malthus. The rest of the matter is simply the issue of who does, and who does not attend that particular pagan church called Anglo-Dutch Liberalism.

The scientific issue posed by Sarpi's Liberalism, is that Sarpi and his followers, such as Rene Descartes, crafted a system among mathematicians, in which mathematical formulations are employed as substitutes for physical principles. Since the modern notion of a physical principle in science has rested chiefly on the affirmation of the method of Cusa's *De Docta Ignorantia*, as that method was realized by Kepler's uniquely original discovery of universal gravitation, there should be no mystery as to why Sarpi, with his avowed mission of employing Ockham as a substitute for Claudius Ptolemy's Aristotle, should have required the invention of the irrationalist myth of empiricism, and why the invention of a virtually mythical Isaac Newton-the-scientist should have been concocted by Paris-based Antonio Conti, et al., to serve, like a stuffed shop-window dummy, as an English-speaking substitute for a nominally French Descartes.

---

treatment of "infinite series," probably done by, or in collaboration with Hooke.

47. The lack of any recorded actually orally uttered statement on science from the mouth of Isaac Newton, is typified by Newton's long-standing position as a member of Parliament. The only oral utterance on record from there, is Newton's "Will someone open a window." There is, curiously, no evidence that former Vice-President Gore was visiting the premises on that occasion.

Art & Science

It were sufficient to look back to the historical origins and persistence of the Liberal (i.e., Ockhamite) Venetian reforms introduced by Paolo Sarpi, including the shift of Venetian maritime power from its former Adriatic base, to the northern European maritime provinces, to recognize the consistency of the principled determination of the nature and practices of the Anglo-Dutch Liberal financier-oligarchical imperial interest, to its present-day expression in the current 2008 U.S. Presidential election-campaign.

Most of the leading actors on that present stage, are to be seen as, to a very large degree, virtual puppets of Paolo Sarpi.

It is therefore of some practical, political importance today, to express decent disgust for the staging of Classical Greek, or modern Shakespearean, Lessing, or Schiller drama in costumes of times which do not correspond to the historical setting in which the original staging of the drama by the author was located. Staging *Macbeth* or *Lear* in times other than those which Shakespeare chose, or, the same for *Hamlet* or *Julius Caesar*, or the same for the great master of the drama, the thorough historian Friedrich Schiller, as above all, his *Wallenstein* Trilogy, is already a fraud perpetrated on the audience. History, in each of its phases of time and place, has a cultural specificity which, as such a specificity, is the essential feature of the drama.

It is the culture which is speaking, and speaking to the actual audience across the intervening actuality of the span of time and place. No decent play is simply the interaction among some actors placed on some stage. The most important feature of any drama is its historically actual place in the cultural history of mankind. The great Classical dramatists put actual history as they knew it, on stage, and put the passions of what they perceived as those times to play out on stage as intended expression of the historical times to which the performance referred. Classical drama must not entertain the audience, but grip the audience to such effect, that, as Friedrich Schiller prescribed, the member of the audience must leave the theater a better citizen than he had entered. To change the historical setting from the actual setting of events, to some other time and place, is an immoral act in and of itself.[48]

---

48. For example, Giuseppe Verdi's transfer of times and places from Sweden, to Boston, Massachusetts was not the intention of Verdi, but of the Italian censor of that time. Shakespeare was exacting in this respect,

That is to repeat a preceding point, respecting such historically specific phenomena as the proposed Lisbon Treaty, that that treaty can not be understood except as the imprint of Paolo Sarpi, as a continuing matrix of culture principle intrinsic to the establishment of what was to become, and has remained the legacy of Paolo Sarpi.

The most significant implication of that same point of historical fact, is that any world-shaking crisis, such as that descending upon all humanity today, can have come into existence only as the overlong persistence of some set of misguided paradigms of a quality simulating axiomatic features of a culture. Thus, as the fate of the world today is largely in the grip of a paradigm established by Sarpi's influence for Europe today. especially Anglo-Dutch Liberal imperial power, so it is against our enemy Paolo Sarpi that the force of our defense of civilization must be focussed.

The world has changed in many ways since the death of Sarpi, but the conflict within the body of the English-speaking institutions, those of the Anglo-Dutch Liberal system and our United States, remains as an essential conflict between what are, virtually, two opposing, relatively immortal systems of society.

It is the axiomatic-like principles which characterize the response-patterns typical of a culture, which remain the determining characteristics of the pattern of developments within, and among cultures as long as those axiomatic-like patterns persist. It is only a seemingly radical change in those axiomatic-like patterns, often, in history, spanning centuries, which determine the history of, and among the relevant nations and cultures.

What remains constant among these patterns shifting in that way, is the essential nature of man, and the actuality of the relative level of development of cultures. The principal changes in the long-wave trends of behavior among cultures, are to be located in the axiomatic-like features. Hence, Paolo Sarpi, although long-dead, typifies the forces which have persisted in Europe since his time, that until we are rid of what he, in principle, represents from our current history's past, as he does, efficiently, still today. The most essential feature of this conflict, centers on that between the

legacy of Sarpi and of the *noëtic* principle. Thus, the conflict portrayed by Aeschylus' Prometheus Bound, remains the principal pivot of historic conflict within the world today.

So, the crucial objective for the future of mankind must be to free mankind and its nations from the grip of institutionalized ideologies such as the slavery of tradition typified by the brutish ideologies attributed to the mythical Olympian Zeus or Paolo Sarpi, and to bring the actual power of human creative reason into play, instead.

IV. The Program of Development

The objective of what is discussed today as "A New Bretton Woods," may be fairly described as an expression of the wish to return to the original Bretton Woods intention of U.S. President Franklin Roosevelt, as if he had not died early during his fourth term in office.

To refresh the reader's memory from the preceding chapters of this report: the regrettable intention expressed by deceased President Roosevelt's successor, President Harry S Truman, was to overturn several among President Roosevelt's essential intentions for the post-war time, especially Roosevelt's intention to uproot pro-colonialist aspects of imperialism from the planet. These Truman actions which were aimed to wreck much of President Roosevelt's achievements, were expressed in chiefly two ways. First, as Truman's intentions to destroy features of those policies which were displeasing to Winston Churchill's anti-U.S.A., British imperialist intentions for the post-war period. Second, to bring that about by aid of forcing a threatened nuclear confrontation with the Soviet Union.

Had President Roosevelt lived to carry out his avowed mission for the post-war period, the entire colonialist and quasi-colonialist systems of European powers would have been liquidated, and Britain itself freed to enjoy a normal national sovereignty under a system of a world composed, exclusively, of an intended system of sovereign nation-state republics.

If we wish to survive the presently onrushing, global economic-breakdown crisis, we, of the United States, must insist on returning to Roosevelt's intentions now. First, we must re-establish the principle of national sovereignty. Then, each presently deprived nation, must be assisted to fulfil its desire to develop into the desired

---

and Friedrich Schiller a true genius. Eugene O'Neill's ***The Iceman Cometh***, passes the test nicely as a case which belongs in my time and nation. Orson Welles' Mercury Theater productions were often the clever machinations of a highly talented and pompous ass.

form of the sovereign nation-state. Not all objectives will be reached immediately, even though they are proper choices; therefore, our policy must be establishing an intended, working system of *developing* sovereign nation-state republics, a goal which must be reached, or else nothing much will have been reached, after all.

As a matter of practice which we are implicitly required to adopt under the present conditions of an on-rushing general breakdown-crisis of the world's present monetary system, the policy of the U.S.A. must become that of replacing the present monetary system by establishing a new Bretton Woods system, as such a design was implicit in President Franklin Roosevelt's efforts through the Bretton Woods conference, instead of the error introduced under President Harry S Truman, of adopting John Maynard Keynes' misinterpretation of President Roosevelt's intention.

The significance of this requirement, is best argued from the standpoint of examining the inherent insanity (and immorality) of the present system of so-called "globalization," as that was the present policy of the Anglo-Dutch Liberal imperialists which was installed during the 1970s. That radical change in direction of the planet's evolution, toward "globalization," away from the U.S. policies of the 1950s and early 1960s, was brought about not only by the August 1971 scrapping of the Bretton Woods system, but by the petroleum-price hoax of the Anglo-Dutch-Saudi operation of 1973 onward, and by the systematic wrecking of the U.S. economy as a whole through the globally radiated impact of the installation of the ruinous program of the Trilateral Commission under the hapless Presidency of Jimmy Carter, and into the 1980s and beyond.

What we of our U.S.A. permitted to happen to our republic, during the interval of the term of Britain's Prime Minister Margaret Thatcher, was tantamount to the influence of treason among us.[49]

---

49. Notable was the policy of the U.S. under Secretary of Defense and George Shultz crony Caspar Weinberger, as in the instances of the Malvinas War of Britain against Argentina and the wrecking of the economy of Mexico during the related State Department operations during Summer-Autumn 1982. The "good side" of President Ronald Reagan showed in Reagan's avowed hatred of a U.S. defense policy based on what Reagan had denounced as "revenge weapons." However, with George H.W. Bush as Vice-President, with Shultz and Weinberger in Reagan's Administration, with Henry A. Kissinger deployed on special missions, and the same Trilateral Commission which had reigned under Carter all over the Reagan Administration, that Administration, in the end, was, overall. a shambles in performance from 1982-1984 on.

The Evil of Out-Sourcing

Back during the 1950s, the bellwether of future disaster was the phenomenon which began to be described, then, as the effects of "run-away shops." What has, subsequently, become a global policy, began to be seen within the United States itself, with the transfer of employment. still within the same corporate structure, from places where higher skills, and relatively higher wages, of a relatively higher-paid quality of labor-force had existed during the World War II times, to areas where significantly cheaper wage-rates and lower local tax-rates (and poorer infrastructure) prevailed. Later, qualitative changes became the prevailing trend, and the export of employment opportunities from the U.S.A. and western and central Europe, to nations with dramatically lowered standards of living.

The more radical change in the U.S.A. came during, and following the 1970s: with the U.S. Nixon Administration's August 1971 wrecking of the Bretton Woods system, the oil-shortage hoax of 1973, and, especially, the 1977-1981 wrecking of the U.S. economy under the Carter Presidency, a wrecking done according to the guidelines adopted by David Rockefeller's Trilateral Commission, led by Zbigniew Brzezinski. The physical-economic conditions of life for the lower eighty percentile of family-income brackets in the U.S.A., have become persistently worse, at a generally accelerating rate, ever since those and related developments of that decade.

To see the result on a global scale, take the case of China.

That U.S. reopening to China which occurred during the Administration of U.S. President Richard Nixon, was not an error in itself; to that degree, it was not only correct, but overdue. However, what should have happened, instead of the lunatic 1971-1972 wrecking of the Bretton Woods fixed exchange-rate system, was the use of the opening of constructive relations with China through negotiating a long-term system of credit under a fixed-exchange-rate system. By that means, we should have acted to emphasize the development of the agro-industrial infrastructure of a developing China economy, that to such effect that a commitment to the full development of the entirety of China's territory and population, should have been the primary objective from the start.

The bad effect of neglecting the latter approach should be clearly evident to competently skilled observers today. The extent of the internal problems in the relatively poorer regions of China today, reflect that fact. The wrong approach taken by the U.S.A. was basing the new relations with China on a "free trade" premise, the policy of inducing China to fulfill U.S. internal consumption requirements at prices far below those which could be matched by production within the U.S.A. itself.[50] Under that misguided premise, especially since 1989-1990, China, like nearly all nations which have experienced expansion of their export industries under "free trade" arrangements since the collapse of the Soviet Union, find that the gain in national income of the developing economy from exports, is not sufficient to sustain more than a minority of the exporting nation's total population and territory. In other words, the exporting nation is losing money on the costs of production represented by the failure to cover the true costs of that national production as a whole. The chief reason for this short-fall is the relevant practice of "free trade," under which China, for example, produces for export at *an incurred true national physical cost* which is marginally greater than the relevant income from export earnings.

This is complicated by the ironical balance of U.S. dollar holdings by China, under the present trend of both the collapse of value of the U.S. dollar on international markets, and the related depreciation of China's current income from exports to the U.S.A. The ugly, medium- to long-term reality of the matter now comes to the fore in this and other ways. A more equitable arrangement between the U.S.A. and China is now needed at a time when the stability and strengthening of relations among the "Big Four" of the U.S.A., Russia, China, and India, is crucial for all mankind.

In the case of China, for example, the problem of underdevelopment of the greater parts of the territory and population is, in itself, a rough measure that China is not paid sufficiently for its exported products to cover the physical costs actually incurred by China as a whole, in producing what represents the net export of China's total production. This is an affliction which infects virtually all of the national economies which have absorbed the production of what was formerly produced in North America or western and central Europe, for sale to, largely, the North American or western and central European nations which had formerly exported the production of these goods to developing nations.

We should have adopted a "fair trade" policy for prices of goods produced outside the U.S.A., instead. It is our failure to continue the U.S. "fair trade," so-called "protectionist" policies of the 1950s which has ruined the U.S.A. in favor of Anglo-Dutch Liberal imperialism, and has created the pattern of crisis and also economic and social disasters among nations exporting cheap products to such places as North America and Europe.

Similarly, since 1989, the former Comecon states, including Russia, have undergone a similar heavy loss on account of the true costs of exports, and of labor, that to the present day. In other words, the apparent "market value" of exports has fallen far below the true costs of production, not only costs of goods, but costs of human life.

In general, the process of globalization, especially as it evolved, since the U.S. stock-market crash of October 1987, during the reign of Alan Greenspan as Chairman of the U.S. Federal Reserve System, has brought about a "globalization-driven" collapse in the real economy of the world as a whole.

The effect of the relevant, prevalent official delusion, on nearly all sides of decision-making, has been that the determined "market price" of goods has been driven far below the true *physical* cost of production by the relevant nation: a policy corresponding to what Soviet economist Evgeny Preobrazhensky of the 1920s called his proposed Soviet policy of "primitive socialist accumulation." Preobrazhensky, during his part in the Preobrazhensky-Bukharin debate of that time, was echoing the rather uniquely competent insight by economist Rosa Luxemburg, and also, later, former U.S. State Department official and historian Herbert Feis, on the specific subject of international loans under finance-imperialist conditions.[51] Otherwise, V.I. Lenin and the German Social-Democrats, like others, had been essentially mistaken in their relevant economic doctrines on the subject of modern imperialism.

These and related facts might seem to be unclear to many commentators, until several points of clarification have been introduced to show the incompetence of

---

50. In significant part, the longer-range purpose of this sort was to shut down the internal market of nations, to make each dependent for a crucial part of its consumption needs on international trade controlled by oligarchical forms of international speculation.

51. Rosa Luxemburg, *The Accumulation of Capital,* Agnes Schwarzchild, trans. (New York: Monthly Review Press, 1951); Herbert Feis, *Europe, the World's Banker 1870-1914* (Harvard University Press, 1964).

Rosa Luxemburg (1870-1919), "the brilliant daughter" of a German labor leader, was right on economics, when the so-called "orthodox Marxists," V.I. Lenin and others, were wrong.

most leading, mostly wrong popular opinion about this matter. For this reason, we must return to subject-matters referenced in some of the preceding chapters of this report.

See how and why the post-1970 policies of the U.S.A. have become such a disastrous, presently global, and terrible failure. Begin with this specific kind of failure in the policies, and the beliefs of the Marxists.

When Rosa Luxemburg Was Right

The mistake of the so-called "orthodox Marxists," V.I. Lenin, and others, who failed where the brilliant daughter of a **Bund** figure, Rosa Luxemburg,[52] had succeeded, has a little-recognized significance for today on precisely this account.

She was not a "Marxist" in the sense of the impact of Marx's doctrines bearing on such matters of econ-

____

52. The **"Bund"** refers to a labor association known in its U.S. extension as "The Workman's Circle." Rosa Luxemburg was the daughter of a notable figure of the association, from Poland, whose career in the Socialist movement was strongly influenced by the French Jean Jaurès whose assassination on July 21, 1914 virtually destroyed what became popularly known as the Zimmerwald movement, so named for a peace conference scheduled to be convened in Zimmerwald in 1915, which was the leading opposition to the unleashing of what was to become known as the impending World War I. Her association with the role of Jaurès was among the most important formative influences of her development as a political figure.

omy as I have just emphasized immediately above. That is to emphasize, that there is no necessarily "rational" relationship between what the so-called "orthodox" Marxists distinguished as "price" and "value." *There is no basis for the assumption that, in a so-called "market economy," there is an underlying, long-term, asymptotic convergence of a so-called "free market," monetary price upon relative physical value. In the entire sweep of U.S. experience since 1968, for example, exactly the opposite has been consistently true for the U.S. economy as a whole.*

The problem with the minds of so many deluded U.S. citizens, is their tendency to prefer to believe, even devoutly, what their masters frighten them into pretending to believe, even when the bitter evidence of experience should have convinced them of the opposite.

The real subject of a policy of "free trade," is not the cheapness of goods, but the cheapness of expendable people, even to the extent of the currently rising, virtually genocidal rise of rates of mass starvation globally, which nothing so much as present, "World Trade Organization" (WTO) policies has done. Such have been among the means for implementing those pro-genocidal policies of Britain's Prince Philip and his World Wildlife Fund, which express his avowed intention to reduce the world's population from more than six and a half billions persons, to no more than two, that in relatively short order of historical time. Worse, that is not only Prince Philip's policy, but had been that of his now deceased accomplice, the Prince Bernhard of the Netherlands who had once signed his letter of resignation from Hitler's SS in the manner he did on the occasion of the date of his marriage to the Netherlands princess. Such is Prince Philip's policy and practice; it is his actual practice, and that of the fraudulent "Malthusian" schemes of such among his lackeys as former U.S. Vice-President Al Gore.

It was thus, also, precisely that, from the inauguration of President Harry Truman, on, in the first instance, and from the relatively much more radical measures of de-construction of the U.S. economy since 1968, which has made the U.S. economy of the 1968-2008 interval the "terminal case" which is expressed by the general breakdown-process of the world economy confronting us all today.

Therefore, it is that miscreant's economic policy-of-practice of Prince Philip and former U.S. Vice-President Al Gore, which is the most important of the globally decisive issues of policy menacing the economy of the entire world, which must be addressed at this point in our ongoing account here. The most relevant way in which to address this issue, is to reference the contrast between the evolution of U.S. economic policy of practice up to the time of the death of President Franklin Roosevelt, in contrast to the lunacy of policy-trends since the assassination of President John F. Kennedy, and, most emphatically, the systemic insanity of political trends in economic policy-shaping which have taken over, more and more, the shaping of U.S. social and economic policy since the end of Winter 1968, and since the approximately coinciding effects, internationally, of the end of the Konrad Adenauer and Ludwig Erhard governments of West Germany, and the virtual ouster of France's President Charles de Gaulle in the same 1963-1968 time-frame.

What Is a 'Fair Price'?

The practice of empire, as illustrated for Europe since Augustus Caesar established that pact, on Capri, with the oriental cult of Mithra, has been the enforcing of the status of what were relatively human cattle, a status which had been imposed upon the great mass of the population of that empire. This policy of practice has been continued by all empires since: by the Roman Empire, Byzantium, by the medieval system dominated by Venetian usurers and Norman chivalry, by the Habsburg-dominated region, and the modern system of Anglo-Dutch Liberal tyranny whose hegemony was defined by the succession of London's orchestration of the so-called "Seven Years War" and the outcome of that war as the British East India Company's imperial triumph in the February 1763 Peace of Paris.

The essential characteristic of the imperialism of these forms, and of kindred oriental forms earlier, has been the denial of the existence of actually creative powers of the individual human mind, as by the legendary Olympian Zeus of Aeschylus' ***Prometheus Bound***. This policy of practice, as it is exemplified by the practice of imperialism, is premised, as by the law of that Olympian Zeus, on forbidding the ordinary human beings to be given knowledge of "fire,"—signifying "fire" as symbolic of those creative powers of progress in knowledge of fundamental physical principles on which the increase of the power of the individual member of society depends, as measurable per capita and per square kilometer of relevant territory.

The practice of empire and its likeness, has demanded the suppression of the actual knowledge of such "fire," and the limiting of access to its use where it is known. In this way, the empire's reign over its subjects, denies them those powers of mental development by means of which they might become willfully independent of imperial and kindred forms of oppressive rule.

Hence, since the maintenance of a certain potential relative population-density must overcome depletion of currently standard resources through scientific and technological progress, the consequent, stupefying—e.g., "Malthusian"—quality of rule by any imperial or kindred system of society is, ultimately, as world-wide now, the perennial source of the doom of empires, such as today's form of the British empire, which have run out of available space to expand. Thus, all empires and kindred systems are doomed by their very continuation in that mode, as the present existence of Prince Philip's pro-Malthusian notion of a British Empire-in-practice, would doom a planet which continues to tolerate such British imperial rule today.

When we consider this prospect from the vantage-point of V.I. Vernadsky's conception of the Noösphere, this cyclical aspect of imperial systems of rule is to be seen as clearly unnatural. Mankind is naturally an anti-entropic species operating within an anti-entropic universe. Thus, the matter of useful price must be considered in these terms of reference.

Consequently, a competent government is impelled to create a "fair price" system, a system designed to conform to the requirement of an increase of potential relative population-density, per capita and per square kilometer of total territory. The solution for the problems this entails was accomplished in the U.S.A. under President Franklin Roosevelt, and was the implied intention of searches in this direction by governments operating in the tradition of what the U.S.A.'s first Treasury Secretary, Alexander Hamilton defined as "The American System of political-economy."

The most significant experience with such an approach to pricing was the U.S. experience with the mobilization for warfare, for which the way was prepared by President Franklin Roosevelt from the first day he entered his first term of office in March 1933, at a time when World War II had been made virtually inevitable by the award of dictatorial powers to Adolf Hitler on the day following Hermann Göring's orchestration of the burning of Germany's Reichstag—a fire which

FDR Library

A competent government, such as that led by President Franklin Roosevelt, LaRouche explains, "is impelled to create a 'fair price' system, a system designed to conform to the requirement of an increase of potential relative population-density, per capita and per square kilometer of total territory." Shown: the President and Eleanor Roosevelt's 1936 whistle-stop campaign for reelection.

was Germany's historic, London-orchestrated predecessor for our experience of "9-11."[53] Roosevelt's Administration was aware of the virtual inevitability, if certainly not in every detail, of a U.S. involvement in such a war. The amount of sheer physical-economic might which the U.S. marshaled and maintained to enable the allies to win that war, is a demonstration of the great economic principle of all modern history, a lesson which the United States appears to have forgotten since the assassination of President John F. Kennedy, and, especially, the death of most citizens of my own generation.

Price: From the Top, Down

To understand the matter of pricing, it is essential to work one's way from the top, down, rather than the bottom, up. It is essential to examine a national economy as a whole, and, then, to examine how that economy does, or should appear, if we were looking from the bottom, up, as we do in looking at the local transaction, rather than the top-down process as a whole.

The first thing to examine is the national productive infrastructure as a whole, from the top down. Then, to examine the process of production of agricultural, industrial, and comparable goods produced. Then, to take into account services such as education, healthcare, and sanitation. Always looking at the economy as a whole— from the top, down, rather than in local detail.

In this view of the matter, our attention must be focused upon the way in which a net increase in productivity per capita and per square kilometer of total territory is effected.

The functional view to be adopted in such a study, is that of attention to the fact that there is an indispensable combination of these, and related component categories, which will determine the net productivity of the entire economy, per capita and per square kilometer. Since there is always attrition, in the forms of attrition of sundry kinds of essential resources, there can be no stability in the economy without a continuing process of scientific and technological progress in the degree required to offset the forces of attrition intrinsic to any fixed mode of technology.

The intellectual function of sundry aspects of public and private policy-shaping is that of what is often termed an "allocation" function. This function, which shapes policy and practice respecting details of activity within the economy as a whole, leads to such included results as the proper roles of taxation, credit, and price. Those roles must be subordinated to the mission-orientation assigned to the economy as a whole, from the top down. Local initiative, as if from the bottom up, smooths out the general policy which evolves from the top down.

"From the top, down" signifies longer capital cycles of investment and consumption, which are largely matters of the functions of international treaty institutions, national governments, local governments, large private

---

53. Adolf Hitler was brought to power by the intention of a complex of financier interests centered on Hjalmar Schacht's sponsor, the Bank of England's Montagu Norman. These were forces including Averell Harriman's Brown Brothers Harriman, and the grandfather, Prescott Bush, of the current President of the U.S.A.

enterprises, learned professions, and so on, down the list, from top to bottom.

In all of these functions, the crucial, needed element of change, is the practice of science and related innovation by individuals and small groups. In general, this requires a predominant role of physical science and Classical forms of artistic culture.

The result of this process of such interactions in the large, includes the matter of local price, and of transactions among individuals and small organizations.

When we inspect a real economy in those terms of references and comparisons, we discover that all of this detail, from the top down, and bottom up, results in a net gain or net loss in the rate of relative physical productivity of the national economy, and world economy, considered as wholes.

The connection among such decisions, at all levels, and in all aspects, results in a measurable estimate of historic values of progress, stagnation, or retrogression. The only competent measurement of performance of an economy then becomes what I have defined as *a potential relative population-density per capita and per square kilometer* of the whole territory and population of a nation, or group of nations. *This is the true measure of economic value.*

Statistical methods congruent with the axiomatic presumptions of Cartesian and related statistical methods are intrinsically incompetent attempted substitutes. People who think in Cartesian-like statistical terms, are therefore intrinsically incompetent as general forecasters. Riemannian dynamics, as a further development of what Gottfried Leibniz introduced as the principled notion of dynamics of modern science, in rejecting the intrinsic incompetence of Cartesian and related statistical methods, points to the foundations of the required methods.

The set of systemic relations I have outlined in the preceding paragraphs can not be competently represented in any formal way not consistent with the concept of a relevant Riemannian manifold. In practice, a good estimate is an acceptable approximation.

Global Fair Pricing

The internationalization of production expressed, in an increasingly significant degree, by "globalization," means that we are approaching a manifest state of world affairs in which the total production by the world is on the way to be less than the costs incurred by the produc-

tion, in all nations, of the world's consumed product. The horror which this presently intended state of affairs portends, is typified by the collapse of the supply of foodstuffs, a collapse which is an implicit expression of failure of the world to meet the true costs of what it produces—the true physical cost of what it produces and consumes.

To the same effect, there has been a general net collapse in basic economic infrastructure in North America and Europe, among other locations, a trend of net collapse of combined wasted and newly built infrastructure since about 1967-68. A collapse of the number of serving physicians, and of hospital and related facilities, in North America and Europe, is an expression of this.

This is to be compared with the monstrously large incomes of a small percentile of the population, who, in net effect, are, like the hedge funds, engaged more in looting, than in even marginal production of useful physical goods and high-quality forms of essential services.

There are many factors of folly which have contributed to this general decline of the practice of physical economy in formerly leading industrialized nations, since about the 1967-68 turn downward in the U.S.A. and Europe, among other places. However, in large part, this decadence of the economies of North America and Europe, for example, has been the cultural effect of the rise into adulthood of the "white collar" portion of the generation born between the close of World War II and the 1958 depth of the 1957-58 U.S. recession. The "anti-blue collar," "anti-industrial," "anti-nuclear power," and "green" traits of that increasingly influential, "white-collar baby-boomer" portion of the population, have exerted an extraordinary influence of the type associated with the lunatic traditions of the Malthusian "machine-stormers" of early Nineteenth-Century Europe, on the political institutions, and other critical aspects of culture, politics, and production of wealth.

The most deadly factor in this complex of ruin which has dominated North America and Europe, most notably, since the riotous days of 1968, has been the influence of the form of mass-insanity typified by the influence, in Europe, of a virtual witches' coven represented by the 1920s and 1930s launching of what was incarnated, after 1945, as a combination of substituting the cult of "information theory" for science, and the operations and influence of the virtually Satanic Congress for Cultural Freedom and the related influence of the British trio of witchcraft's Aleister Crowley, H.G. Wells, and Bertrand Russell.

These forms of economic cultural warfare against modern civilization, combined with the Malthusian campaign, by Britain's Prince Philip, et al., for reducing the world's population from over six to two billions living human individuals, or worse—a much greater genocide than Adolf Hitler's, has been, in combined direct and indirect ways, the greatest single motivating force for the spread of economic and cultural depravity which has gripped the world increasingly since the late 1960s.

Thus, through economic policies of those who promote today's policies of "globalization," and through the cultural policies, such as those of the former Congress for Cultural Freedom, we have driven the net price of production below a less than zero-growth economic standard of living for a great portion of the world's population at large, and, even worse, have been using these means for driving down the per-capita physical productivity of the existing world population (of more than six and a half billions persons) toward what Britain's Prince Philip insists must become no more than two billions.

The true physical cost of production, contrary to those evils of currently intended practice, is the cost of maintaining the entire human race in a rising standard of physical productivity per capita and per square kilometer. The true value of goods and services produced is therefore to be determined as the standard of living and productive culture, required for the planet as a whole, per capita and per square kilometer.

The Role of Language-Culture

The present goal of what is advocated as "Globalization," is the transformation of global civilization into a gigantic, new "Tower of Babel,"—i.e., tower of babble.

As the experience of our U.S.A. "melting-pot" nation illustrate the point, the efficient definition of culture is not a specific language, but, rather, a language-culture: a group of languages in use, assembled around a principal national language. That means, as the best aspects of U.S. culture illustrate the point, that there is a national language of record for legal and related functions, but the language is a kind of bench-mark for the

set of secondary, family tongues of which the population is composed; that legal language serves as the pivot for unifying, rather than "ghettoizing," a language-culture of the population as a whole. The multiplicity of languages associated with a central language-culture, is not a drain on the language-culture of the people, but, rather, tends to force the raising of the cultural level of the population as a whole.

The principal source of unprofitable quarrels about the matter of a national language-culture, so defined, is the kind of ignorance which is spread through attempts to standardize speaking and writing in such a way as to limit the meaning of words, sentences, and paragraphs to a strict, dictionary codifying of meanings, as by aid of a rigid style-book. The New York Times Style Book is case in point.

The characteristic of the mental development of the individual human being is associated with the principle of Classical irony, as the case of William Shakespeare, Percy B. Shelley, and John Keats, typifies this for the use of the English language by intelligent speakers. It is through irony, and only through Classical conceptions of irony, that the creative powers of the mind generate and impart creative expressions among literate users of the same language, or language-culture.

This significance of Classical literacy in art, is ultimately the same as the distinction of the crippled mind of the literal worshipper of mathematical formulas, from the competent scientific thinker. The crippled mind locates the idea in terms of the equation; the intelligent citizen sees the formula as a mere shadow of a universal physical principle, as the work of Bernhard Riemann illustrates that point.[54]

The literally deductive mode of thinking, whether in physical science, or in practice of grammar, is not only the mark of a self-damaged mind, but is a practice which damages the human mind by crippling the individual's native potential for true creativity.

We already see the ongoing process of "globalization" as crippling the potential of the individual subjected to the effects of a tendency toward a "Tower of Babel" as a substitute for a literate language-culture. It

54. "… Es führt dies hinüber in das Gebiet einer andern Wissenschaft, in das Gebiet der Physik, welches Wohl die Natur der heutigen Veranlassung nicht zu betreten erlaubt." From Riemann's 1854 habilitation dissertation, *Über die Hypothesen, welche der Geometrie zu Grunde liegen*, **Bernhard Riemanns Gesammelte Mathematische Werke**, H. Weber, ed. (New York: Dover Publications reprint, 1953).

is the enriching of the use of the creative powers of the individual mind, through the promotion of the powers of creativity associated with irony, on which the progress, and the morality of society depend.

V. Phaedo: What Is Immortality?

The time has come, in the writing of this report, at which I should speak for myself.

The greatest of all of the commonplace failures of societies thus far, has been the failure to grasp the actual implication of the common theme of ancient Plato's **Phaedo** and the writing on the subject of that great work by modern Moses Mendelssohn: the true implication of the immortality of the mortal individual's human soul. Unfortunately, most among even those who profess to seek immortality, do not see it as a continuation of something uniquely specific to human life, but, rather, with the prefatory remark, on the anticipated brink of death, "And, then?"

For the rest of mankind, they are so gripped by their own fearful prescience of human mortality, that they do not even suspect the purpose in mortal life which they should be seeking. The best part of them, is the fearful sense that it is something like that which they should be seeking.

Simply, the animal aspect of the individual denies itself such knowledge; but, what is called the soul remains as it was, always there, as I have spoken and written on past occasions, as if continued life of the soul might suggest the assembly of souls, from assorted past times, portrayed by Raphael Sanzio's **The School of Athens**.

The problem has been, that most people, still today, (empiricists, for example) do not believe that they actually possess a "soul," except as a Sunday-go-to-meeting dress which they have borrowed for the occasion. There is a reason for this phenomenon; that is, that the victims of such an induced outlook treat themselves as loyal subjects of what Aeschylus portrayed as the Olympian Zeus of the **Prometheus Bound**. They accept the obligation to deny the actual principle of human individual creativity which is the difference of man from beasts, as a quality which does not lie within the bounds of the mortality assigned to the beasts. They accept the status of virtual cattle, which British empiricism, such as that of slave-trader John Locke, assigns to people. They accept the view of that willing slave, who does

"Mankind is so gripped by their own fearful prescience of human mortality, that they do not even suspect the purpose in mortal life which they should be seeking." Raphael's "School of Athens" (1510), in the Vatican, portrays the principle of immortality. Shown: a detail, with Socrates (second from right), in dialogue with other members of the Platonic Academy.

not create, but, rather, like the believer in the swindle called "faith-based initiative," hopes for good things—especially money, or what it might buy—to be caused to descend upon him.

So, where truth is known, great accomplishments in national economies, when they occur, often have a "life" in the order of a century or more. Important developments in development of power-systems and essential investments in productive facilities, have economic lifespans equal to those of a contemporary human generation, or longer. The development of the technologies required for progress, requires the dedication to producing such effects over several successive generations. The mission of society on these accounts is immortal, as one generation produces a successor, and another successor generation after that. We teach our young, if we are sane and moral, the premises of the accomplishments which will be realized by our children and grandchildren.

Yet, those discoveries of universal physical principle which have generated all of the great improvements, live on, eternally, as the goodness from which relatively long-lived man-made benefits, as of a generation or more, live on temporarily for our advantage.

Thus, on those premises of experience, alone, we should suspect that the human individual, as distinguished from the functions performed by the member of the animal species, is immortal.

A Hellish Fact, or Two

I have explained this earlier in this report, in emphasizing the specific legacy of Paolo Sarpi as the central feature of the Anglo-Dutch Liberal characteristics of British Liberalism today. In the case of the history of British Liberalism since its emergence around Sarpi during the last decades of the Sixteenth Century, we are confronted with a form of mental-moral disease typified by moral-intellectual stagnation, as in the shift from Marlowe and Shakespeare to the depraved circles of Bacon and Hobbes. In the happier variety of cases, we would expect a high rate of conceptual progress from generation to generation.

When we consider the poverty which reigns in most of entire continents, such as in Africa and Asia today, and when we also consider the types of known remedies which are required to overcome these conditions, a moral society is to be defined in terms of centuries of its commitment to foreseeable goals of general development of the quality of not only the productive powers of labor as such, but the creative powers of the individual human mind. Thus, our departed ancestors live in us, as we should live in the improvements, as changes, which we have transmitted to our descendants.

When we define the term productivity within those terms of reference, we experience a qualitatively different definition of individual and general morality than when we think of the narrow interest of individual life between the bookends of birth and death.

We may come close to the truth of this matter, when we speak of "immortal" works of art, such as the crafting of that cupola of Florence's Santa Maria del Fiore by Filippo Brunelleschi, which was the first modern definition of the use of the catenary as a principle of physical design, later defined by Leibniz's demonstration of the universal principle of physical least action.[55]

---

55. Paolo Sarpi's hoaxster Galileo Galilei, for example, never actually knew what a catenary (the funicular curve) is, although he claimed to know.

A true demonstration of a universal principle is Johannes Kepler's discovery of the universal principle of gravitation as such, in his *Harmonies*, as being a true universal physical principle; the argument of Albert Einstein on the uniquely valid universality of Kepler's discovery, as the prototype of a truly universal physical principle, is relevant.

Immortality is not "a thing," but a principle of the universe, for which certain objects are predicates. Immortal principles of the sort which typify the human soul as a being distinct from all forms of merely animal life, lie in the progress of accumulated knowledge of the human mind, powers accumulated through transmission of those living conceptions, that by aid of re-experienced acts of such discoveries. The great concrete works of physical science and Classical artistic composition, are footprints of the passage of those principles. It is through the replication of such acts of discovery of universal principles, that the immortality of the human soul is efficiently expressed. The footprints of that movement of the creative human soul, are what is more famously recognized as key to locating the works produced by the immortality of the human soul.

The common difficulty, even among elegant individual minds, is the fearful seizing upon the mortal act which expresses a footprint of immortality, for the actual foot which leaves that print behind.

The true statesman, of the special type we require for conquering the great challenge now before us, recognizes, and acts upon that specific distinction of the spirit which moves the true hero, by the current effect which the spirit has expressed. A long life, of men and women who have contributed great acts, is good; but, immortality is all that is truly enduring. Such men and women are the true immortals from among our species.

Those of us who are so persuaded, adopt as their life's immortal mission, service to the future of mankind. It is that self-interest which we defend. It is that self-interest which we refuse to betray.

There is a great mission presented as a challenge to present-day mankind. That is a mission to accept the distinct sovereignties of the people of respective nations, with no attempted "Tower of Babble" permitted. The function of the existence of each sovereign people, is all future mankind.

The signs are clear. These terrible times now immediately before us, warn us to unite, as respectively sovereigns, to defend the proper common aims of mankind.

Anthony Wentworth Morss, 1931-2018: A Life-Long Contribution to Art

All improvement in the political sphere is to proceed from the ennobling of the character—but how, under the influence of a barbarous constitution, can the character become ennobled? We should need, for this end, to seek out some instrument which the State does not afford us, and with it open up well-springs which will keep pure and clear throughout every political corruption.

I have now reached the point to which all the foregoing considerations have been directed. The instrument is the Fine Arts, and those well-springs are opened up in their immortal examples.

—Friedrich Schiller
On the Aesthetic Education of Man, Ninth Letter

Aug. 26—Anthony Wentworth Morss died at the age of 87 in New York City on August 6, 2018. Maestro Morss was known to most as a meticulous and passionate opera, choral, and orchestral conductor, but to those who had the privilege of knowing him and working with him closely, he was a personal inspiration: Maestro Morss was always teaching—in almost every conversation—in the realm of music, of history, and of the highest Ideas. At the same time, he always saw himself as a student of what was new to be learned in Art and in Classical culture. He credited his over thirty-year association with Lyndon and Helga LaRouche with revealing to him the real, living Friedrich Schiller, whom he regarded as his personal hero and Ideal.

Maestro Morss, the artist, musician, and conductor, came from a long line of New England industrialists and military engineers. His forebears were among the early settlers of Newburyport, Massachusetts in the 17th Century. Charles Anthony Morss founded a small wire manufacturing company in 1841 called Morss & Whyte. In about 1885, when Thomas Edison was lighting the first electric street lamps in New York City, Morss & Whyte moved into the production of insu-

EIRNS/Stuart Lewis

Anthony Morss

lated electric cable. The family business, later named Simplex Technologies, Inc., was to play a large role in U.S. defense communications in World War II, and today is a world leader in transoceanic fiber optic cable research and production.

With this as background, Tony Morss would often relay the story from his student days at Harvard College, when he "broke the news" to his father that he planned to make a career, not in the family business, but as a musician. His father's reaction was shock, dismay, and the strongest disapproval. However, Tony was not to be dissuaded from his early path towards becoming either a concert pianist or conductor.

In an interview published in the *Koussevitzky Recording Society Journal* in 1995, Tony Morss recalls that at age eight or nine, he attended a symphony concert for the very first time at Boston's Symphony Hall, conducted by its director, Serge Koussevitzky, who concluded with Tchaikovsky's Sixth Symphony (*"Pathétique"*). The experience shaped his life and career: "The whole experience was absolutely magical, riveting.... Much of what I heard went over my head. What I did hear was something that was thrilling, something that was tremendously important in ways I did not fully comprehend—and an enormously emotional experience. The conductor seemed to be absolutely spent and so did the orchestra. I later discovered the orchestra really felt this way."

Later, at age fourteen, through a friend, young Morss was invited to spend a weekend with Koussevitzky and his family at his home near Tanglewood. Tony drank everything in, and later noted that "People who knew [Koussevitzky] much better than I, and who spent hours conversing with him, were always astonished at how well-informed he was, at the breadth of his interests, whereas somebody like Toscanini was so exclusively focused on music that he was, I would say, considerably less informed...."

While still a student, Tony Morss was chosen by Leopold Stokowski to be his Choral Master and Associate Conductor for his Symphony of the Air. Later he became the Music Director of the Majorca and the Saragossa Symphonies in Spain. He was especially proud of the mixed professional and amateur choruses which he directed there. These choruses toured the country under his direction, winning praise and prizes in many competitions. Maestro Morss was Music Director of the Norwalk Symphony and Chorus Master of the American Opera Center at Juilliard in the United States. He guest conducted the Madrid, Barcelona, Cape Town and Marseilles symphony orchestras as well as opera companies throughout the United States. He counted well over one hundred operas in his working repertoire.

In 1990, Maestro Morss conducted a concert version of Beethoven's opera *Fidelio*, performed at the Verdi tuning of A=432 Hz, in conjunction with the Schiller Institute. Maestro Morss was a tireless public advocate of a lowering of the current, arbitrarily high tunings to the scientific pitch of approximately A=432. He recruited other musicians to this requirement on the basis of, firstly, the urgency to stop the physical destruction of young voices, and secondly, the requirement that Art must be beautiful, an impossibility at the elevated tuning. In the recent period, Maestro Morss was working on solving the technical challenges of allowing all the instruments of the Classical orchestra—including the woodwinds—to play at the Verdi pitch on modern instruments.

When the Schiller Institute NYC Chorus was first formed in 2014, Maestro Morss became one of its greatest advocates and a loyal stalwart in the Bass section.

The chorus was enriched by his voice, but even more so, by his constant presence. As the chorus grew in size and renown, new singers and players would come to their first rehearsal, see Maestro Morss' tall presence in the Bass section, and say, in effect, "Well, if Maestro Morss is in this chorus, this must be on the highest level." Maestro Morss loved the joy and the work of bringing the greatest art to large New York City audiences, many of which comprised young people who were "new" to Classical music. Recently, he would often remark that singing in the Schiller Institute NYC Chorus was "certainly the greatest experience of my entire life!"

Maestro Morss served as the Music Director of the New York State Opera Company, the Verismo Opera, the Asociacion Pro-Zarzuela en America, the Eastern Opera Theater of New York, and the Lubo Opera Company of New Jersey. He served on the executive board of the Foundation for the Revival of Classical Culture, which is dedicated to the education of young people in the principles of composition and discovery in Art and in the Sciences. He received the Lifetime Achievement Award for his twenty-year role as Music Director and Principal Conductor of the New Jersey Association of Verismo Opera in 2015, and in 2018, he received the first Walter Damrosch Award from the Musicians Club of New York.

Maestro Morss was lucid and compelling in his insights to his last breath on Earth. In our last conversations with him, he talked at great length and specificity about Beethoven's life and his compositional method in the *Ninth Symphony*, Schiller's breakthroughs in military science as conveyed to Russia's Czar for the military defeat of Napoleon's army, and of the significance for history of the individual whom he called, "that greatest polymath, Lyndon LaRouche."

A good many years after the young Tony Morss angered his father by choosing a life for Art, his father traveled to Spain to hear him direct a symphony orchestra. Yes, his father happily agreed, then, with Maestro Morss' early wisdom: to devote his life to what Schiller called "the instrument [of] the Fine Arts."

A Memorial Service will be held at 11:00 a.m. on Saturday, September 29, 2018 at St. Ignatius of Antioch Episcopal Church, 552 West End Avenue, New York, N.Y. In lieu of flowers, please send donations to The Musicians Club of New York, 360 Cabrini Blvd., Apt. 1D, New York, N.Y. 10040.

—Richard A. Black